P9-CQP-387

Coffee Cup, Friendship & Cheesecake Fun

Becky Freeman

HARVEST HOUSE PUBLISHERS
Eugene, Oregon 97402

Published in association with the literary agency of *Alive Communications, Inc., 7680 Goddard Street, Suite 2000, Colorado Springs, CO 80920*

Cover design by Kochel Peterson & Associates, Minneapolis, Minnesota

COFFEE CUP FRIENDSHIP AND CHEESECAKE FUN
Copyright © 2001 by Becky Freeman
Published by Harvest House Publishers
Eugene, Oregon 97402

Library of Congress Cataloging-in-Publication Data
Freeman, Becky, 1959-
  Coffee cup friendship and cheesecake fun / Becky Freeman
    p. cm.
  ISBN 0-7369-0291-0
  1. Female friendship. I. Title.

BF575.F66 F69 2001
158.2'8'082—dc21   00-053844

To the AttaGirls

Lunching, laughing, and sharing our friendship
is what makes this journey in writing,
speaking—and life—such joy!

"No man is a failure who has friends."
—Clarence, the angel in *It's a Wonderful Life*

Contents

Chick-Chat

Part I
First Aid Friends
When Good Friends Are Better Than Therapy

Part II
Two Gals Are Better Than One
When She's the Other Half of Your Brain

Part III
Bring Out the Pom-Poms!
Cheering Each Other Through Terror and Triumph

Part IV

Let's Hear It for the Boys!

When Guy Friends Rate up There with Girlfriends

Part V

Kindred Spirits & Big Bosom Buddies

Experiences That Connect Us Heart to Heart

Acknowledgments

How grateful I am to have settled into Harvest House Publishers as one might settle into a friend's living room. Because so many of the employees at Harvest House are women, it's truly like a girlfriend party when we get together. (With apologies to you Harvest House guy friends whom I also appreciate more than I can say. But, hey, this IS a girl's book.) A big hug to all who turn these words on paper into real books, then do the hard work of getting its message out to those who may be blessed by its contents. Particular thanks to Carolyn, LaRae, Betty, Hope, Teresa, Kari, Brynn, Julie, Laura, and Carol Ann. If I've left out a Harvest House Babe involved in this project, please forgive me and know it is due to a scattered, often absent, mind.

I've dedicated this book to my amazing network of writing friends, the AttaGirls, who not only encourage my writing heart, but are there for every crisis in which one might long for a real, caring group of friends. This week, my father—having had heart surgery—called to ask me who the AttaGirls were. They'd rallied together to send him a Get Well bouquet. Blessings to Brenda, Gracie, Cheri, Lindsey, Rachel, Lynn, Suzie, Rebecca, Fran, Kali, and Ellie. Also a special thank you to my amazing assistant and friend, Rose Dodson; mentors and friends, Gene and Carol Kent; and over-the-picket-fence friend (and part-time "Mom" to Gabe), Melissa Gantt. Thank you to my mother and father, Ruthie and George, and also to my father- and mother-in-law, Jim and Bev, who applaud and pray for my every undertaking.

And finally, to my agent, my dear brother, Greg Johnson, who strolled into my life a few years ago and casually handed me his expertise and his friendship and then begin steadily sending me Fed-Exed packages of paper dreams about to come true. You are holding one of them in your hands right now. Thank you to my other Colorado Guy Friends as well: Chip MacGregor for making me laugh out loud on blue days and Lee Hough for making me feel intelligent on days when I feel I've literally misplaced my mind.

My offspring are growing from children to adult friends, and this year has brought the particular joy of welcoming Zeke's wife, our new daughter-in-love, Amy, into our fold. Thank you, kids, for your patience, love, and unending cheerleading, and for being so enthusiastic about the one hot meal a week I manage to cook.

My husband, Scott—the years we've shared are bringing a tenderness and depth to our married friendship that is surprising and delightful to me. After all this time, Babe, you're still the one.

Finally, to you my reader-friends who write me and say, "I feel like I've known you all my life" and who ask eagerly when the next "Becky Book" is coming out. You keep me writing with joy!

I warm myself in the fire of the friendships that surround and support me.

God bless you, everyone.

Chick-Chat

This morning, my teenage daughter did her best to help this middle-aged mom look as cool as possible (given the fortysomething material she had to work with). I strutted out the front door in black platform, strappy sandals, black slacks, a white lacey T-shirt, and a lime green, below-the-hip jacket. Rach had pulled my hair up in a loose French twist and secured it with Oriental chopsticks, then garnished it with tiny green and pink flowered bobby pins. With freshly done acrylic nails and matching toenails (painted "juicy watermelon"), I don't mind telling you I was feeling pretty with-it and groovy. (My daughter, peering over my shoulder, just informed me that any hopes I'd had of actually being a cool person were just dashed by my word choices of "with-it" and "groovy." I do try.)

Why this sudden urge to depart from my regular uniform of whatever I can find in the laundry room that doesn't have to be ironed? Because, girlfriends, I was going on TV to hang out with three other totally cool women. The hostess of the show, Jenni Borsellino, could enter and win any peppy, Barbie look-alike contest; however, she's down to earth, compassionate, and funny so we have no choice but to love her anyway.

The talented producer of "At Home-Live!"—this energetic, daily, live show—is Trish Ragsdale, who is equally as adorable as Jenni, only a little shorter. (She could be Barbie's little sister, Skipper.) Trish, blond and wearing a "pleather" jacket and burgundy pants, looks all of 23 years old, but swears she's 37. I want to see her birth certificate for evidence. (Keep in mind that Trish doesn't have children yet, and I think your body ages about five years for every child.

9

So I tell myself I'm not doing too shabby. When you add in my Birth-giving Depreciation Allowances, I should have the body of a 60-year-old. And I'm lookin' GOOD for 60.)

Now, Jenni's hubby, Chuck—her usual, moustached and charming TV sidekick—happened to be out of town; and while Chuck was away, Jenni decided to play. So she invited some girlfriends over to the studio for the day.

Jenni even coaxed Trish from her behind-the-scene director's chair to in front of the camera. This, I must add, was not an easy transition for Trish. She really likes being in charge. She normally gets a whole space to herself where she can whisper orders into TV hosts' ears, via a hidden microphone, and they robotically follow her every command. (I ask you, is there a more perfect place for a control freak to work than in a cubicle called "The Control Room"?) But somehow—probably by bribing her with chocolate—Jenni got Trish out of Control and onto the set.

Next, the irrepressible Thelma Wells, of Women of Faith fame, strolled onto the set decked out in a stylish red and black suit with some snazzy shoes that Jenni began to covet almost immediately. Then Yours Truly (Woman Who Runs With Women Cooler Than I) joined Trish, Jenni, and Thelma for the first ever "Girls Only" hour on "At Home-Live!"

The show opened with the most important girlfriend ritual of all. Thelma and Jenni whipped up a rich, deep, dark chocolate cake. (When Jenni asked what sort of dessert Thelma and her husband, George, liked to cook up on a typical evening now that they were empty nesters, Thelma just silently raised her expressive eyebrows and gave a "Wouldn't you like to know, Child?" grin that could have melted cold butter.)

Then Trish and I went to the overstuffed living room set to gab about pampering ourselves—Trish drinking herbal tea in antique china cups by candlelight; me pulling out a hammock, a pillow, a book, and a quilt to demonstrate my original gourmet napping techniques. Since I find writing to be relaxing, I showed the audience a pretty little book where I record all my deep thoughts so my children can have them when I die.

"So that's about all the room you need for your deep thoughts, huh?" Trish asked, pointing to the tiny, slim volume. I had to admit, sheepishly, in front of thousands of viewers that not only was my *Deep Thought Book* the size of an average deck of cards—it actually has plenty of blank pages left. "Maybe I ought to change the title from *Mom's Deep Thought Book,* to *Shallow Thoughts from a Wee Little Mind,*" I offered.

The second half of the show found all four of us gathered 'round the kitchen table laughing, praying, drinking tea, eating chocolate, and talking and giving out free advice that would make Dear Abby proud. After the show, we were all feeling refreshed, like little girls again, as if we had played all morning in unselfconscious fun rather than performed.

"Why is that?" Trish wondered as we walked out of the studio and down the hall.

"It's the girlfriend thing," I answered. "It's just refreshing to be with other women, no men around. Especially when we are talkin' FUN women."

"Which, of course," Jenni added with a knowing nod, "we are."

If you're a woman, you know exactly what I mean. (And if you're a man: What were you *thinking,* opening this book about cheesecake and coffee and girlfriends? Did you even think of knocking on the cover first? And what of your macho reputation? Well, if you've made it this far, you might as well keep on reading. It's your big chance to be the proverbial fly on the wall at a girl gab party in book form.)

Have you noticed that most women tend to run in packs? Whether they run with the wolves, or prance with French poodles. It doesn't really matter. Women just want—and need—a bunch of female friends to lie in the sun with, go out for food with, and howl over their babies with. It's what we do. Who knows why?

If I could create my own job, do you know what I'd be? Seriously. I'd be a professional friend. I'd do breakfast with a funny friend over coffee (I need humor to get me going in the A.M.), then I'd write notes to friends who need encouragement or help with a project. By noon I'd be ready for lunch with a group of creative writer friends. Then I'd need a few hours of alone time to nap and rest my mouth. By late afternoon/evening, I'd be ready to shop or go to a movie or browse a bookstore with an artsy friend or maybe hang out on my back porch with an easygoing neighborly friend. If only I could get my friends to pay me for showing up, this could *work*.

From *Little Women* to *Steel Magnolias,* I'm drawn to stories centered on female group bonding. I think this is because I know, from personal experience, that it takes a variety of friends, each uniquely gifted, to bring a rich wholeness to life that I crave. I imagine we are all jigsaw puzzles with little parts of us missing: small flaws, things we don't do very well (organize, cook, remember birthdays); or places where we hurt or need comfort or an infusion of another's joy.

Then a certain friend comes along and fits into that little open place, making our life more complete, and suddenly we realize how much we'd been missing that connection, that little puzzle piece.

Perhaps you're melancholy and appreciate that friend who understands and affirms your depth and moods. She makes you laugh and brings a much needed playfulness to the lunch table.

Or perhaps you're the go-get-'em, hard charger who discovers a friend who is sensitive to beauty, who reminds you to slow down and enjoy the present moment—before you charge your way into the brick wall of burnout.

If we don't judge each other, but instead give generously out of our own giftings—and receive graciously what our friends offer us, we find ourselves wrapped up in something priceless, something eternal. Not only that, but we give our friends the profound gift of *feeling needed*.

I recently read with fascination that biochemists are now saying that each cell in our body appears to have been created for bliss. Even the tiny one-celled animals seek out pleasure sources voraciously. As it turns out, the most powerful joy-producer, the ingredient that makes our cells shout "Hallelujah!" is good relationships.[1] Really! Looking under a microscope, scientists can see that stronger than any drug, mightier than any quick thrill, is the power of good, happy, consistent, people-to-people connections.

Want to be truly healthy and happy?

Forget the rice cake and tofu diets.

Find, develop, nourish, and cherish relationships with your family and friends.

In pondering how to write this book, I asked myself, "Self? Is there any one Have-All, Be-All Friend you could write about?" And I had to admit, no one woman (or man) can be the Everything Friend, although some come awfully close. I've discovered that nourishing many different kinds of friends is important; it's truly doubled my joy and halved my sorrows. There's always SOMEONE available when I'm in crisis or ready for some fun. This storehouse of friendship, like most things worth having, has taken years of give and take; years of showing up; years of being there for others, too. But I cannot imagine anything more worth the effort.

You may have a group of girlfriends nearby that you've loved and enjoyed for years and you purchased this book in celebration, or as a gift. Or perhaps you've just moved to a new place and are feeling a little lost today, longing for a lingering coffee cup conversation—and you've bought this book as a temporary surrogate friend.

Either way, you've come to the right place. Why not make a cup of Earl Grey or take this book to a great little coffee nook and order a slice of cheesecake if you're feeling daring! Or better yet, whip up "Angel Amy's Cheesecake" (recipe starts on the next page). Then settle into an overstuffed easy chair, dive into these pages, and join me in some lively, hilarious, tissue-dabbing, chit-chatty, too-much-fun-to-do-housework-today girl talk!

A man who has friends must himself be friendly....
PROVERBS 18:24 NKJV

"The person who treasures friends is solid gold."
—Marjorie Holmes

Angel Amy's Cheesecake

(Courtesy of Leslie, the delightful owner and innkeeper of The Enchanted Country Inn Bed & Breakfast in Eugene, Oregon. This is the BEST cheesecake I've ever tasted!)

Crust:

1 ¾ c. graham cracker crumbs
⅓ c. butter—softened
1 ¼ c. sugar
¼ c. chopped nuts
dash cinnamon and nutmeg

Filling:

2 ½ lb. cream cheese
1 ½ c. sugar
¼ c. flour
2 T. lemon zest
½ t. salt
½ t. nutmeg
1 T. brandy or 1 t. brandy flavoring
6 eggs
½ c. whipping cream

Topping:

1 ½ c. sour cream
3 T. sugar
1 T. brandy or 1 t. brandy flavoring

Soften cream cheese while preparing crust.
Crust: Mix all ingredients together and
press into the bottom of springform pan.

Beat cream cheese until fluffy. Stir together sugar, flour, lemon zest, salt, and nutmeg. Blend into cream cheese. Beat together brandy and eggs, then gradually mix them into cheese. Take care not to overblend. Stir in cream. Pour into crust and bake at 325 degrees for 1¼ to 1½ hours.

Leave oven door ajar and cool cheesecake one hour.

Spread on topping and chill.

Part I

▲ ▼ ▲

First Aid Friends

When Good Friends
Are Better Than Therapy

1

"Let's Go to the Movies!"

Chick Flick Friends

There are chick flicks and then there are chick flick *friends*. And you don't really get the whole Chick Flick Enchilada without both ingredients.

For to go to certain films without at least one good girl-friend along is like watching a movie without hot buttered popcorn and an ice-cold Coke. There's just something about a communal movie-watching experience—no boys allowed—that is revitalizing and therapeutic. And, as my son Gabe is prone to say, it's just "flat-out fun."

To tell the truth, it wasn't until my neighbor/friend Melissa introduced me to the joys of a girls' movie day that I understood its importance to the feminine experience. She has so thoroughly convinced me now, that it has become our custom to take a Chick Flick day about every two months. (Preferably driving to Dallas where they have those great cushy chairs piled up theater style.) Then we eat Chinese food from a buffet until we're ready to pop. The perfect female bonding experience.

Last month Melissa telephoned and said, "You know, we live next door, and I haven't seen you all summer."

"I know," I wailed. "I've been overwhelmed with deadlines and travel and I've felt a little like the neighborhood hermit. Help!"

"Can you be ready at 6:35?"

"Yep."

"All right then, I'll honk and you come a runnin'."

Within the hour I heard gravel crunch under the wheels of Melissa's car, said a quick good-bye to the family, grabbed my purse, and darted out the door. Then I stopped dead in my tennis shoe tracks.

I could not believe what I was seeing right before my eyes. There, in a white Mustang convertible, sat Melissa and her daughter, 13-year-old Sarah—their hair blowing in the breeze, arms bent at easy angles against the car doors, summer sun glinting like diamonds over the whole Elvis-beach-movie scene.

I hopped into the back like a teenage girl. "How'd you finagle the keys from Josh?" I asked with a laugh. Joshua is Melissa's teenage son, the owner of the sporty Mustang.

"Easy," Melissa said with a wink. "I waited until he said something smart-alecky."

"Which didn't take long," Sarah volunteered brightly.

Melissa shrugged and then finished her sentence. "Then I grounded him from the car and asked for the keys. What do ya think?"

"I think you are a bloomin' genius. Let's go for a ride!"

I loved the whole convertible, moms-driving-a-Mustang scene: the wind blowing my hair, the stereo pumping out a pop tune, three girls escaped from the prison of sameness, free and on our way to the movies!

That night we saw *Where the Heart Is*—a great, Southern-style chick flick. The three of us grumbled aloud about the jerk of a guy who left his pregnant girlfriend in Wal-Mart (reminiscent of the days audiences hissed at the villain in melodramas) and cheered quietly as scene by scene justice was served and the poor mother found a new life and true love. Very satisfying film, as chick flicks go.

When we see comedies, Melissa lets go with a laugh that makes me laugh harder than the comical scenes before us warrant. It's sort of a snort-snort-guffaw, snort-snort-guffaw, and the more she tries to control it, the snortier it gets until I could care less about the movie. The real entertainment is Melissa's guffaw and the unbelieving looks of people sitting around us.

We've learned to bring Kleenex along if we hear the movie is sad, because neither of us can be trusted to restrain our tears if the film hits strong emotional chords. During one chick flick date with Melissa, I can still recall one scene from *The Story of Us* as if it were playing in front of me even now. A classical guitar (playing "Classical Gas") is being strummed hard and urgently in the background. Poignant scenes are flashed on the screen to the rhythm of real marriage: wedding day, births of babies, steamy kisses, slammed doors, bored looks, moments of terror and sadness and exquisite joy—all jumbled together in one brief but masterful, mini-musical collage. Rarely have I been so moved—for the couple's story was way too much like watching our own Marriage Past in all its angst and glory. When the lights came up in the theatre, Melissa and I glanced at each other, looking for the entire world like a pair of overwrought raccoons with smeared mascara for eye patches. It wasn't the first time we'd given in to the depth of feeling that only comes with a good, hard cry.

In my book *Real Magnolias*, I highlighted a story about the time Melissa gave a neighbor's little girl the gift of life—in the form of her own kidney. But by way of introduction to our particular brand of friendship, I recalled the time we went to see another movie together.

Melissa had badly broken her foot that summer and was confined to a cast and crutches for three full months. In addition, it had been one of those difficult seasons with extended family crises coming faster than Melissa could handle them. I wrote, "Have you ever had a time in your life when you felt the world was raining down so hard and so fast it almost hurt to wake up in the morning and walk out life's door? In times like these, we tend to forget the light in our lives, the joy we were born to give, the great things God once worked in and through us and will work again. At the core of whirling pain, we are desperate to latch on to who we are, and why we are here—to anything that feels like hope."

It was during such a time in Melissa's life that we chose to go see the movie *Hope Floats*. Thankfully, we'd stopped at a convenience store to stock up on tissues. Melissa hobbled through the theater on crutches while I followed behind with purses and popcorn in tow.

During several of the movie's more poignant scenes, I dabbed at my eyes—but when I looked to my left, Melissa was nearly convulsed in tears. So quickly was she soaking tissues, I offered her the last half of my packet, whispering, "You just let it all out. You've earned a good cry." She smiled weakly, blew her nose, and reached for another tissue.

"I mulled over the two-word title of the film for several days," I wrote about that experience, "appreciating more and more the life-affirming message it sent. For even when human beings, and our own bodies, fail us, God's gift of hope is ever resilient, finding its way to the surface of life's pain-filled ponds."

Movies, indeed, have incredible power to bring pictures, music, story, and dialogue together in a way that gives vent to bottled up human emotions. Of course, the more fragile we are as moviegoers on any given occasion, the more we're moved by scenes on the big screen. I think it helps, if at all possible, to have a girlfriend along for the after-movie therapy session, while your feelings are still near the surface—before your mind talks your emotions out of feeling deeply. Or at the very least, give yourself some after-movie down time. In fact, one woman psychiatrist recommends to her clients who've become numb to their emotions that they go see an emotion-packed movie like *Schindler's List, My Life, Braveheart, Good Will Hunting* or *Steel Magnolias.* Then she urges them to go straight to their car after the movie, do not pass Go, and holding on to the images they've just seen, sit in the privacy of their car and let go with any emotions they're feeling. She found that movies reach places in the heart that therapists sometimes cannot, or will not, go. And they draw latent emotions to the surface where they can finally be faced and healed.

There was a time when my Christian counselor friend, Brenda, and I wanted to write a book about the powerful, therapeutic, and healing effect of movies on women's lives. For whatever reason, it didn't seem to be God's timing for the book to become a reality—though I think both of us would like to re-visit the concept some day. In preparation for the proposal, I wrote of a time when my own emotions were raw and tender. And how a movie, *The Horse Whisperer,* seen in the company of friends, affected me deeply. On this particular occasion, Brenda and I had invited our husbands along for the fun, and later that night I wrote in my journal about the whole experience as if I were re-living it in my mind…

It is good to be here, I think, as I ease into my cushioned seat, letting my neck muscles relax. My husband, Scott, and I are meeting Brenda and her husband, Frank, for a night out at the movies. We've all looked forward to seeing *The Horse Whisperer*.

As the theater darkens and the movie comes to life with the rich tapestry of characters, music, and scenery, I find myself longing to dissolve into many of the scenes—especially the ones of a slower-paced life, or majestic beauty, or warm family moments around picnics and campfires. And yes, okay, the scenes of Tom (played by Robert Redford) slow dancing, in his boots and softly faded jeans, aren't too shabby either.

I glance to my right and snuggle close to my husband, whose quiet, knowing demeanor and rugged ways remind me of Tom. If Scott had been a cowboy, I believe he'd have been the whispering, listening-to-horses sort. I peer to my left now and again, and in the dark I catch glimpses of Frank and Brenda chuckling or wiping away a tear or sharing a comment. As we scoop popcorn from the same giant-size box, passing it back and forth among the four of us, we also share visual scoops of the story unfolding before our eyes in all its Technicolor brilliance—of beauty beyond description, pain beyond words, sensual desire beyond satisfaction, healing beyond bounds.

When the movie ends, and the credits roll, Brenda and I make our way to the ladies room, which by now is overflowing with women. (It was a three-hour movie—all bladders have been stretched to their fullest capacity.) Behind me, Brenda whispers, "That was soooo good. I am speechless." But, as it turns out, there's a speech in her after all. "There's just so much in that movie to talk about...."—the ladies in line visibly lean towards us to catch snatches of this post-show ladies room commentary—"Did you pick up on the pressure the daughter felt to be special, to be perfect?" I nod. Both Brenda and I were children of high achievement, having performed much of our lives to secure the favor of others. At midlife, we are struggling to be okay with just being okay.

Brenda continues excitedly, "And there was even pet therapy in there—Gestalt Pet Therapy!"

"Only a therapist would say something like that," I say, squeezing her in a friend-hug as we both laugh. *And only you would say it with such childlike joy*, I think, as I smile. Brenda often squeals with delight when she happens upon new and interesting thoughts, like a little girl who suddenly discovers a perfect shell on the beach. It's one of the things I love most about her.

Exiting the movie theatre, we find our husbands and decide to head to town for a bite to eat to extend the evening. Once in the restaurant and comfortably seated in a corner booth, I note with surprise that we don't begin talking right away about the movie's plot or characters, or discussing its meaning. The movie itself is not mentioned.

But from the moment we place our order with the waitress, our conversation grows deeper, as if the tender mood of the movie—its essence—still lingers. I speak of some of the pain I'm walking through as I struggle to find peace with a tender issue. I fight back tears until I lose the battle and they spill over anyway. "I'm confused about a lot of this," I confess, feeling very small and vulnerable, hoping someone will change the subject to something else, like dessert.

Brenda pats my hand from across the table and says, "For whatever it's worth, I think you are one of the most psychologically healthy people I know." It's worth a lot. I lift my eyes and smile weakly, gratefully. Frank too is listening, as is my husband. Three pairs of eyes, filled with compassion, focus on me. I'm not accustomed to being the hurting one in the spotlight, surrounded by this much listening.

I think of how Pilgrim, the wounded horse in the movie, has to relive a past trauma in order to heal. In the presence of the accepting horse whisperer, he is allowed to buck and rear up, and finally, fall helplessly to the ground with the pain of it all. Here in a quiet corner of this restaurant, my friends are letting me cry without shame, hearing me buck and flounder, and finally, fall softly to my emotional knees.

When Pilgrim allows himself to lie down, Tom urges the young Grace, Pilgrim's rider, to come close, and to soothe the horse with gentle, comforting strokes. Grace comes. Grace heals. My friends stroke me gently with their affirming words, with touches on my hands, which lay folded, downed, and helpless on the table.

I am in the presence of people whisperers.

I have been broken and blessed.

Larry Crabb once wrote, "Our hope is in community. Sometimes that community will be most experienced in a counselor's office, sometimes over lunch, sometimes with a group of folks watching a movie together..."

Dr. Crabb shares insights worth embracing, for I've seen women friends and men friends alike drawn together in community under the flickering light of a movie screen.

Brenda and I once hosted a Girl's Night Out for the ladies at our church where we simply got together, drank coffee, and watched the movie *Enchanted April* together. Then we talked about the rich, redemptive themes in this film about a group of English women escaping their gray lives for an Italian holiday in living color. We soaked up the lingering beauty of the dialogue and scenes, one after another, as a collective whole. It was a special evening.

Do you need a break from the days of your life but don't have time for a real vacation? Take a day off, call up a girl-friend and ask her to go with you to celebrate your freedom with a movie and lunch out. Are you carrying around pent-up emotions and want to cry, but can't seem to get started? Rent a surefire tearjerker video and have a bunch of girl-friends over for a rip-roarin' Sap Fest.

Because the stereotypical chick flick isn't just something to laugh at.

It is a wonderful something to cry at, too.

Just don't forget the popcorn and plenty of tissues.

> *Even in laughter the heart may sorrow....*
> PROVERBS 14:13 NKJV

"Movies take the common crystal of human experience, cut it, polish it and hold it up to the light of a 35-mm projector so that those sitting in the dark can see it sparkle, and leaving the theater, take something of that sparkle with them."
—Ken Gire, *Windows of the Soul*

Some of Becky's Favorite Chick Flick Picks

(Movies I Want My Daughter to See, Now and in the Future)

Enchanted April: I love this movie for the scenery (great escape movie for the wintertime blahs) and the powerful reminder of how grace can change our lives and relationships.

Little Women: I wonder, is it me, or do all women identify with restless, wannabe-a-writer Jo? Moms, there's a wonderful scene in this movie where the mother is combing her daughter's hair and says something profound about inner beauty versus outer beauty. Somebody rent the movie and remind me what that profound thing was, would you?

Steel Magnolias: The scene after the funeral is masterful, provoking that rarest of emotions and an unforgettable line: "Laughter through tears is my favorite emotion."

My Fair Lady: What girl doesn't love watching a makeover? To my surprise, Scott and our teenage sons actually rewound this movie to replay Rex Harrison's famous, "Why Can't a Woman Be More Like a Man?" song. Apparently his confused-guy thoughts are timeless, even to the more modern, but still mixed-up, male minds.

The Sound of Music: I know every word to every song and grew up dreaming of being a nun who would forsake her vows to fall in love with a handsome, uniformed man and make clothes out of curtains for his orphaned children— punctuating these events with frequent, spontaneous bursting into song. (I also know all the tunes in *Oklahoma!; The Music Man;* and *South Pacific.*)

Gone With the Wind: Scarlett may have been rotten, but I can't deny she was fascinating to watch. We admire her spunk even as we despise her selfishness. There's probably more of Scarlett in us women than we care to admit. (Fiddle dee dee.)

Seven Brides for Seven Brothers: When I was a young girl, I loved this old musical about seven rugged mountain brothers being tamed by seven potential brides. Though my daughter made fun of it at first, she stayed with it to the end and replayed it start to finish for her girlfriends.

On Golden Pond: Katherine Hepburn has some lines in this movie about living with less-than-perfect people, coping with a less-than-perfect childhood, and loving a less-than-perfect life that are at once true, transcendent, and tender. The "you're my knight in shining armor..." speech is one every wife needs to give her husband when the world pulls the shades down on his life.

Coal Miner's Daughter: Sissy Spacek and Tommy Lee Jones were flawless in this performance. The early scenes of Loretta Lynn's girlhood and young marriage to "Doo" are priceless in their humor and authenticity. I recently reviewed this old favorite, and had a new appreciation for the scene where Loretta is about to collapse on stage and says, "Patsy Cline used to tell me, 'Little gal, you got to run your own life.' But lately, my life's been runnin' me..." This hit a little too close to home after a much too busy season "on the road" and caused me to make some decisions to more carefully guard my time with my family.

First Knight: I believe that the Camelot story is much like a fairy tale version of Eden. King Arthur is like God; Lancelot and Guenevere are like Adam and Eve who betrayed the King they loved by falling into temptation. The King gives his life to save the betrayers he loves. Camelot, that "shining city on a hill," is Eden Lost, and the memory of it is the heaven we long for. Watch this well-made version of the King Arthur tale and look for Christian themes throughout the story.

Fiddler on the Roof: This movie, as rich in music as it is in family emotion, provokes all sorts of memories. Scott played the rabbi in his high school play, and my father sang, "Sunrise, Sunset" at our wedding. A month ago, Scott and I and my mom and dad sang "The Sabbath Prayer" to celebrate my son Zeke's marriage to his bride, Amy.

Honorable Mentions: *African Queen; The Quiet Man; It's a Wonderful Life; White Christmas.*

Refreshing Cake

(My daughter's friend Cricket and her mother, Janice Cowley, served this one Sunday afternoon to a bunch of girls. We were hooked and have been baking it for every girlfriend occasion ever since—from slumber parties to birthdays to after-movie wind-down times.)

1 box yellow cake mix
4 eggs
⅔ c. oil
11 oz. can Mandarin oranges with juice

Icing:

1 small can crushed pineapple
12 oz. Cool Whip
Large box instant vanilla pudding

Mix first four ingredients. Batter will be lumpy. Grease and flour oblong cake pan. Bake at 325 degrees for about 30 minutes or until done.

Cool and chill.

Mix ingredients for icing together with a wooden spoon or mixer. Ice cake and keep in refrigerator. Serve cold.

Yuuummmmmmmmmyyyy.

2

"I Missed You!"

Welcome Home Friends

Yikes! Where is that blasted cell phone?" I yelled aloud as I dug through the covers of the hotel bedspread and over-turned the contents of my purse, a make-up kit, and a tote bag in a desperate search for the source of the ringing.

I finally found it, stuck between an open tube of lipstick and a compact. Breathless, disregarding the oily streaks of red lipstick rubbing off the phone and onto my hands, I flipped open the tiny phone's cover and managed a fairly articulate, "Hello?"

"Becky," the voice said in a tone usually reserved for fed-up mothers. "You've been gone way too long. It's time for you to come home now!"

"Oh, Gracie...you don't know how badly I want to! Brenda just left me the sweetest message on the hotel answering machine about missing me. Y'all are too much! But I've got a whole week of this exciting, non-stop glam-orous media tour left to do."

"Beckles, something's just not quite right when you are gone this long."

I swallowed hard, missing my two best buddies almost as much as I missed my kids and my husband. We even have silly names for each other. Gracie calls me Beck or Beckles. Brenda is Brendy. And Gracie is—well…ummmm? Just Gracie. I made a mental note to work on a cute nickname for her as I sat cross-legged on the bed and took a sip of in-room-coffee-maker coffee. It tasted like warm liquid plastic. "It's horrible to be away this much, and, Gracie, I'm so tired—just don't know how I'll make it. But it sure is nice to hear your sweet bossy voice."

"So, where are you?" Gracie asked.

"Right now, I'm at the Embassy Suites in Los Angeles, and I could kiss the floral print carpet. Wait 'till I tell you about last night. Can I cry on your long-distance shoulder for a minute?"

"Sure, Hon, you just let it all out."

The next best thing to a therapy session—perhaps BETTER than therapy—is a sympathetic friend willing to let you bend her ear now and again. "Okay, well…you know that in the last month I've been in Georgia, Missouri, Alabama, Louisiana, Indiana, South and North Carolina, Chicago, Toronto, and Winnipeg and…"

"Oh, Beck," Gracie interrupted. "I can't keep up with your schedule. It gives me a headache. But didn't you e-mail me that you almost got arrested in Canada? What happened?"

"Oh, yes! That's when the border patrol asked to examine my suitcase. Even before she opened it, she put on a pair of rubber gloves, which I thought was pretty insulting. Then when she unzipped my luggage, I could tell right away, by the way she grimaced as she gingerly picked her way through my packing, that she was glad she was thoroughly latexed. I asked her if my suitcase was the messiest she'd ever seen."

I smiled as Gracie's low chuckle poured from my minia-ture tele-link to home. Though I'd balked at cell phones at one time, I'm now so grateful for their ability to beam me back to the voices of loved ones. "What did the border patrol lady say?" Gracie asked.

"She said, 'Well...hmm...yes, I think there was one other set of baggage a little worse than this that came through here a couple of years ago.'"

"Oh, no!"

"Oh, yes. And then—this is where my heart stopped—she picked up a little Ziploc baggie of white, powdered Meta-mucil from the tossed salad of my wrinkled clothes. All I could think of was how was I going to explain to Scott that I was being held in a Canadian prison for possession of a laxative."

"How did you get out of that?"

"I showed her the book I was going to talk about on TV the next day and told her it was about all the dumb things I did without thinking ahead. Things like packing cocaine-looking powder in a clear plastic bag and putting it in my suitcase and traipsing blithely across the border into another country."

"So she believed your story?"

"I don't know if this is a compliment or not, but it didn't take her long, after listening to me stammer excuses for a few minutes, to announce that she thought I probably posed more of a threat to myself than to Canada."

"So what happened last night?"

"Oh, yeah, last night. Well, I arrived in L.A. and took a shuttle to a hotel booked by the producers of this TV talk show. Turned out it was in one of the more dangerous sections of

L.A., so I was already a little nervous. And when the reservationist tried to explain the complicated series of directions to my room, I had to get her to draw a map. It was behind the main building, just beyond the dumpsters, over the concrete bridge covering the back parking lot, up an old elevator and down a dim hall. But once I managed to get there without being mugged, I had to admit—it did have a lovely view of a seedy back alley."

"You've gotta be kidding…"

"I know! I was thinking: Hollywood—swimming pools, movie stars. But it looked more like the Clampett's cabin. The bathtub was rusted-out porcelain, and the furniture was nailed-to-the-wall yellowed Formica. I don't know which was more threadbare—the carpet or the bedspread. There were double doors with metal edges and big glass inserts—almost like sliding glass doors—opening to the outside with a flimsy little lock to hold them together. It was a breaking-and-entering dream."

"What did you do?"

"I took a bath and changed clothes for my interview, then called my wonderful Harvest House publicist and told her she could take the money out of my royalties or my hide, but that I needed to change hotels so I could be sure I would live through the night to catch the next plane and the next interview. She was horrified about the situation and said, 'Becky, just pack your bags now, go to the taping and then we'll get you in another hotel tonight.'"

"Well, that was awfully nice of her," Gracie duly commiserated. And even though I knew she didn't call just to listen to my sad story, she graciously fed me another question. "So how was the TV show?"

I took a sip of plastic coffee and dove into Part 2 of My Whining. "Well…I was to meet the show's driver in the hotel lobby at 3:30 P.M. By 4:30 P.M. he had still not arrived, so I began calling every number I had with me to find out what had happened."

"What time was the show supposed to start?"

"Five o'clock! I finally got hold of the producer and asked her what happened to the driver they were sending. She said, 'Becky?' and I said, 'Yes...' and she said, 'Becky Freeman?' and I said, 'Yesssss...' and she said, 'Ohmigosh, I thought you were here already. Oh, dear—we've been thinking the other guest's wife was YOU all afternoon.'"

"Uh-oh," Gracie said.

"Uh-oh was right. The producer hurriedly said, 'Listen, Becky, we're sending our driver to the hotel. He's short with dark black hair. Hopefully he'll get you here in time for the last segment.' So a few minutes later, this short man with dark black hair and a Middle Eastern accent walked into the hotel lobby. He smiled and nodded at me, and I smiled and nodded at him. I asked him if he was my ride, and he said, with all the confidence of a man in charge of the universe, 'Jes, I AM jour ride.' So off I went with him."

"Becky, you aren't going to tell me you went with the WRONG man are you?"

"Gracie, you know me too well. After about a mile of conversing with this man, whose name I found out was Simon and who hailed from Armenia, I realized he had no idea what TV show I was talking about or where in the city of L.A. we were going. Thankfully, Simon turned out to be a pushy, over-confident but friendly taxi driver and not a serial murderer."

"Becky, do you realize how many angels you are wearing out?"

"Oh, listen, my angels must have been on double duty yesterday. There we were using two cell phones and speaking two languages—with me intermittently laughing in English and Simon alternately laughing with me and then pausing to holler at other cars in Armenian. Somehow, we miraculously arrived at the TV station just in time to tape a last-minute segment. They just put me on the set, powdered my nose, and told me to say something witty. I was really tempted to describe the events leading up to my staring at the television cameras like a 'coon caught in the headlights, but I restrained myself."

"But you made it through the show, and I'm sure you charmed them all."

"I have no idea if I charmed the audience or simply stunned them. My mind's sort of blank about it all. When the show was over, Simon—who seemed like a good buddy by now—was waiting for me in the parking lot. He opened the door to his green-and-white taxi with a flourish and said, 'I just call my wife and tell her about you! She say, "That poor lady in this crazy city. If she have no place to stay tonight you bring her home…"'"

"You didn't…" Gracie's mothering antennae alert system had been activated.

"No, no," I assured her. "I told Simon I appreciated the offer, but that I'd love nothing more than to be dropped off in front of the safe, brick-enclosed, well-guarded entry to the Embassy Suites hotel."

"And there you are!"

"And here I am. Gracie, right now I feel like shouting, 'God bless hotels with inside-only room entrances.' There's room service and a microwave and plush carpet and two TVs where, if I choose to do so, I can watch news stories of the latest local drive-by shootings from the living room and the bedroom at once. And…" I paused, swallowing hard.

"And?"

"And I'd give all the chocolate mints I've ever had on fluffed-up pillows to be sittin' cross-legged in a booth at Taco Bueno with you right now."

"Well, come on home, Hon."

"I'm comin' just as soon as I can get there."

"Becky, remember, Brenda's got her deadline coming up." I knew what this meant. Brenda and Gracie and I are not only close friends but we meet every two weeks to edit each other's manuscripts. The unspoken rule is that when one of us is a week away from a deadline, we all pitch in to help the highly-stressed writer make it through the intensive labor before her due date. It's like promising not to be too far away when your best friend is ready to give birth to her child. Book deadlines involve just about as much hand-holding and heavy breathing and hollering. Only difference is—you give birth to a cereal-box-sized square of stacked, typed paper instead of a seven-pound infant.

"Don't worry, Gracie. Tell Brenda I'll be there three days before her book is due."

A few days later, I did three shows in one day in Toronto. (I remembered NOT to bring powdered medication in little baggies into Canada this time, but managed to lose my birth certificate in the airport! Again, bless my angels, the border patrol waved me on, saying, "You don't look capable of lying." I swear, if anyone needs an undercover agent, I'm the middle-aged woman for the job.) After a long day and evening of talking and traveling, I arrived at Dallas-Fort Worth Airport at the woozy hour of 2:00 A.M. (Plane delays due to bad weather had stopped air traffic for four hours. These are the experiences that turn seasoned businessmen into large cranky toddlers. I found myself asking my seat-mate, a computer technician who looked as if he were about to switch from pouting to crying, if he wanted to borrow my airplane blankey.) Upon arrival on Texas soil (concrete concourses in this case), I struggled up five flights of stairs with my luggage in tow, thinking all the while, *Lord, I'm so glad to be in Big D. Just give me strength to drive one-and-a-half more hours to Greenville…*

When I finally, blissfully, located my minivan in the dim glow of the long-term parking lot lights, I sat down on the curb and wept. Not because I was beyond exhaustion, not because I was overjoyed to be almost home, but because my front driver-side tire was flat as a Jersey cow patty.

My dear sweet husband came out in the middle of the night and changed the tire, then we both drove home just in time to see the sun come up through our red, squinty mole-like eyes. Less than 24 hours later, I had to take another plane to speak at a three-day conference in Kentucky, then home for one day, then two days in Dallas doing television shows. (Thankfully, blessedly, my daughter, Rachel, got to join me in Dallas! And she was willing to do a house call—since my house, that spring, seemed to be on the road.)

Thus ended two months of a "glamorous" author tour, coupled with a dozen previously committed speaking events. (Next year I may have myself pre-committed—to a local mental hospital—if I ever take on this much traveling at once again! One author friend, Stormie Omartian, told me that at one point during her glamorous tour of publicity-duty, she called her publicist and exclaimed, "I'm not a Fed-Ex package!")

On Friday afternoon, I walked in the door of my country home-sweet-home and sank to my knees in gratitude for the sheer gift of being on my own messy carpet, close to my husband and kids and friends and the post-office people who know me by name.

Within 30 minutes, I heard familiar voices giggling and making their way from my front door toward the back porch. I fell into the embrace of two women friends so dear to my heart: Gracie and Brenda.

"Welcome HOME!" they both said in unison as we joined arms in a female friends-forever version of the football huddle. We spent the whole luxurious afternoon catching up on our personal soap operas, laughing at each other's antics, editing Brenda's manuscript, and eating out at the local cafeteria surrounded by a deep blue-haired sea of senior ladies. Brenda lifted her iced tea in a toast. "We made it! With your help, I think I'm going to live through this deadline and Becky lived through a book tour and Gracie lived through both of us complaining non-stop and we're all together again!"

Being with my best friends was more refreshing than a massage and a hot bath and a long summer's nap all together. Over my humble platter of almond crusted cod, steamed spinach, carrot salad, and a nice hot wheat roll (what Gabe deems "old folk food"), I realized just how right Dorothy of Oz had been. "There's no place like home, there's no place like home…" As long as home is where your best friends are waiting for you, demanding that you slow down to play with them awhile —and, preferably, begging you to never go away for so long again.

> *…Every time I think of you in my prayers,*
> *which is practically all the time,*
> *I ask him to clear the way for me*
> *to come and see you. The longer this waiting*
> *goes on, the deeper the ache….*
> ROMANS 1:9,10 THE MESSAGE

*"Best friend, my wellspring
in the wilderness!"*
—George Eliot

*"Friends minister to each other, nurse each other.
Friends give to each other, worry about each other,
stand always ready to help. Perfect friendship is
rarely achieved, but at its height it is an ecstasy."*
—Stephen E. Ambrose, *Comrades*

Simple vs. Real Friends

A simple friend has never seen you cry.
A real friend has shoulders soggy from your tears.

A simple friend doesn't know your parents' first names.
A real friend has their phone numbers in her address
book.

A simple friend brings a bottle of wine to your party.
A real friend comes early to help you cook and stays late
to help you clean.

A simple friend hates it when you call after he has gone to
bed.
A real friend asks you why you took so long to call.

A simple friend seeks to talk with you about your problems.
A real friend seeks to help you with your problems.

A simple friend wonders about your romantic history.
A real friend could blackmail you with it.

A simple friend, when visiting, acts like a guest.
A real friend opens your refrigerator and helps himself.

A simple friend thinks the friendship is over when you
have an argument.
A real friend knows that it's not a friendship until after
you've had a fight.

A simple friend expects you to always be there for them.
A real friend expects to always be there for you![2]

Becky's Best "Welcome In from the Cold" Southwestern Chili

1 lb. ground beef, cooked, crumbled, drained of fat

1 large jar good quality, chunky spaghetti sauce
(I like Mom's brand with chunks of garlic and basil, made with all natural ingredients, no sugar)

1 can lean chili (I use Health Valley's Spicy Black Bean Veggie Chili)

1 can red kidney beans

1 can shoepeg corn

1-2 T. honey to taste

Tony's Cajun Seasoning (I use this on everything!)

Sour cream or Tofutti's Sour Supreme for you lactose-intolerant gals

Chopped green onions

Mix first seven ingredients in a large pot and simmer until it's the thickness you like!

Top with a dollop of sour cream and chopped green onions.

Great sprinkled with croutons and grated cheese. Serve with tortilla chips or cornbread and dinner's done!

Just wait for the compliments. ☺

3

"Wanna Go Ride Bikes?"

Playful Friends

As I whistled my way out the front door and mounted my almost new $79.95 purple bicycle, I couldn't help thinking to myself, *I've finally found MY sport! An athletic activity I can actually do—and enjoy!* I loved riding my mountain bike up and down the tar-covered roads that meander around the lakeshore where we live. There's one particular break in the road that takes me back to carefree girlhood—a tree-covered path where you have to ride up and down an impressive dirt hill before your wheels connect with paved road again. If no one were watching, I would often take that downhill run—the breeze blowing my hair behind me—with an audible, childlike "Wheeeeeee!"

Occasionally, while riding around, I'd run into my favorite neighborhood kids: seven-year-old twins named Nickie and Lindsey and their slightly older brother, Alex. Then we'd ride in a pack together, like Maria and the children in *The Sound of Music*. Once, when Lindsey and Alex had taken the lead, Nickie and I fell behind, both of us struggling to get up a steep hill. I glanced over at Nickie and smiled some encouragement his way. His blond hair was wisping around in the wind when, with the wisdom of Solomon, he announced thoughtfully, "Going uphill is a test. Downhill is a reward." Since that spring afternoon, I'd often pondered his poignant observation.

But this particular afternoon, I was riding solo, without the benefit of small philosophical companions. I peddled as fast as I could on the uphill test of the ride in order to reap the reward of a good downhill "Wheee!" But as I crested, an enormous black dog the size of a small elephant, with a shark-like grin and a vicious bark, leaped out of the woods and lunged toward my Nikes. Not knowing what to do, but desperate to avoid losing a hunk of my calf to Jaws-on-Four-Legs, I quickly determined to take the offensive.

I steered in the direction of the dark, barking enemy and...well, the upshot of my quick action was—I ran over the dog with my bicycle. The deep, junkyard bark faded to a Chihuahua-sized yelp, and I suppose the dog ran off to the woods either in surprise or humiliation. I can only *suppose* this because everything went sort of black in my head after the initial impact of middle-aged woman, bike, and dog. Other than the sound of the high-pitched yelping, the next thing I remember is lying face down on the road, one arm awkwardly and painfully outstretched over my head. My sole thought was, *I am dog food.* But apparently, the dog had wounds of his own to nurse, though I'll never know if they were physical or psychological in nature, as he was never seen or heard from again.

It's interesting the things one does when one thinks one is going to be eaten alive by a giant dog or, at the very least, run over by a large truck before one can gather the wits to stand up. I'd always assumed I would cry out to God in such a state of helplessness. Looking back now, I also wonder why I didn't shout ugly words in the general direction of my four-footed attacker in an effort to scare him off and save what was left of my skinned-up limbs. But I did neither of these things. What I did was yell, "Scott! Scott! Help me!" This made absolutely no sense because I knew I was a good half-mile away from home. When I'd left to go riding, Scott had been napping in the bedroom. Not only that, but I was around a ninety-degree corner—our house was nowhere in view. So really, what were the chances he'd see or hear me?

Still, whatever obstacles we've had in our marriage, I've always been certain of one thing: Scott would rescue me if I needed rescuing. If Scott had been a cartoon, he'd have been Superman; if he'd lived in pioneer days, he'd have been Dan'l Boone. And so the fact that Scott could not possibly hear me did not keep some stunned, primitive part of my brain from believing my hero's supersonic ears would pick up the cries from his lady-in-distress.

And, indeed, that's exactly what happened. At the same time I managed to stand up and flag a passing motorist down with my one good arm, Scott was already walking out the front door to look for me—in response to a sudden, uneasy feeling he had that I might be in trouble.

"Oh, Babe..." he said gently as he helped me out of the Good Samaritan's rescue vehicle. "What happened?"

"I ran over a dog with my bicycle," I offered—only it came out sounding more like a question than an answer. Scott looked at me and then at the young Good Samaritan couple who drove me home and said, "She's in shock, isn't she?"

A few ice packs later, I was sitting in the emergency room next to my hero, waiting to find out how much damage I'd done to my right arm. It was July 3, and a sort of pre-Independence Day madness had apparently seized the town, because the emergency room was soon filling up like a popular restaurant.

I sat across from three well-muscled Hispanic men dressed in sleeveless T-shirts and assorted black leather accessories. I'd assumed they were waiting around for a buddy who'd been knifed or hurt in a motorcycle accident. I smiled at them and asked who they were waiting for. Scott cleared his throat. It always makes him nervous when I'm friendly with gang members, but I was really curious. One of the men, with a bandana around his head, said, "My little boy has a fever. He's back there with his mama." Turns out the whole lot of them were related, and, as is so often true in Mexican culture, where one member goes, the whole family follows. In fact, they quickly introduced me to Grandma who was knitting in the corner.

When the burly men saw the extent of my cuts, scrapes, and bruises and the impressive swelling of my right upper arm, one of them asked. "How'd you do THAT?"

By now I had my explanation on auto-reply. "I ran over a dog with my bike."

The gang looked duly impressed. One of the younger guys, with a Harley tattoo across his bicep and four rings in his lips, asked, "What kind of bike you ride, man?" I hemmed and hawed a bit, then lifted my chin and answered, "The kind of bicycle you get at Wal-Mart for $79.95." Scott looked toward the ceiling as if he'd dearly love to take flight.

My reply kept the three leathered men in hysterics for the better part of the next 15 minutes. But it wasn't long before I was upstaged by a teenage boy with a swollen arm and startled eyes stumbling through the emergency room door.

Us biker types turned our investigative eyes in his direction. "What happened to you? Was your arm in some kind of explosion, man?" one of my compadres inquired, hopefully.

The young man nodded, bewilderment clouding his eyes. "I was," he said. "The air bag went off in my car."

As a generally concerned mother-at-large, I compassionately asked, "Were you in a car accident, Honey?"

"Sort of," he answered. Then he sheepishly confessed the whole sordid truth. "Actually I ran over one of those parking bumps in an empty parking lot." This entertained the emergency room gang for another 20 minutes. The teenager who'd been air-bagged just barely finished his story when yet another young man walked in with a perfectly round wound on his head—like a giant ringworm—centered just above his eyebrows. Turns out he'd made a home-made firecracker out of a PVC pipe—which, in turn, had propelled itself right into the middle of its creator's forehead.

I was feeling better about myself with each turn of the revolving door. I nodded toward the cast of waiting room characters as if to say to Scott, "See, I'm not the only odd duck in the pond."

Eventually I left the entertainment of the waiting room to get X-rayed and examined. A short while later, Scott was by my side nodding in empathy as the physician showed him the two X-rays of fractures to my upper arm. (Ironically, and I think, insensitively, the doctor referred to this as my "humorous" bone.) Since the bone did not need to be set and since doctors don't fit casts around upper arms, I was sent home with a prescription for pain relief and orders to see an orthopedist within the next few days. The attending physician decided to spare me the physical pain of removing the hospital gown that the X-ray tech had wrestled on me earlier. Instead, he inflicted the mental pain of duct taping the gown closed at the back and having me parade back through the emergency waiting room looking like a character in one of Jeff Foxworthy's books. (You know you're in a redneck ER when they send you home in a hospital gown wrapped in duct tape.)

If Norm Cousins, of *Anatomy of an Illness* fame, is right, and laughter is a relief for pain and a balm for trauma, I served as human codeine for at least half a dozen victims that night, simply by showing up.

I say this with pride: the bruise that appeared on my right arm the next day was easily the most impressive contusion I've ever seen. I was mostly solid black and blue from my shoulder to my elbow. Since I had been on an all-pain-killer diet for 24 hours, floating on a cloud of perpetual medication, I wasn't feeling too shabby, all things considered. In fact, this is truly the highpoint of an injury: when it looks astoundingly awful, but you are too drugged to feel any actual pain. You get tons of sympathy and pampering and you can take three daylong naps without a shred of guilt. Running over a dog with your bicycle does have its perks, however short-lived.

We'd planned to have friends out for the Fourth of July, and since my arm would be broken whether they came or not, we chose to party on. (Every year, folks who live and weekend-cabin around us load up boats, barges, and beer and meet in the middle of the lake to watch fireworks explode from the shore. Typical of Southern priorities, the homeowners around here may not be able to gather funds to fix potholes in the road, but we INVEST in firework displays.)

So there we were, about a dozen of us of various ages, shapes, and sizes—floating along in our dilapidated barge, a plastic American flag whipping in the wind at the stern. Now and again the dark sky would burst forth with outrageous, spidery displays of color. I looked over at the young daughter of one of our friends. Chelsea is about six years old, with a charming lisp and a perpetual look of wonder about her face—the sort of expression one might imagine on a cherub.

She paused for a moment during a brief period of silence between firework explosions and then looked at me and my bandaged arm with the compassion of a miniature Mother Teresa. I'd recited the tale of the dog and the bike to her and anyone else who would listen earlier in the evening. Chelsea had been fascinated and curious as to how a grown-up person could have done so much damage by falling off of a bicycle. She shifted her eyes to Scott, whose hero arm was draped protectively around my ailing shoulder. "Mr. Scott," she asked earnestly, "did you take Miss Becky's twaining wheels off ?"

Scott simply, sadly, nodded his head in the affirmative.

"Oh," my young friend replied, with a knowing, faraway look in her eyes. Without saying a word, I could see that she was mulling over the terrifying risks involved in becoming a rider of a training-wheels-free bike.

▲ ▼ ▲ ▼ ▲

How I wish I could spare all my little friends from the reality of Life Without Training Wheels. A life where terrifying black dogs can jump out of nowhere and nip at your heels and make you fall and get hurt really badly.

But I'd also have to describe the dizzy freedom of life on a training-wheels free ride—the wind blowing through your hair, the world whizzing by, lost in the joy of "Wheeeeeee!"

Alas, life is a test. And a reward.

Just like riding a bike.

Jesus said, "Let the little children
come to me...for the kingdom of heaven
belongs to such as these."
MATTHEW 19:14

"*There's no friend like someone*
who has known you since you were five."
—Anne Stevenson

Growing Up with Our Friends

In kindergarten, your idea of a good friend was the person who let you have the red crayon when all that was left was the ugly black one.

In first grade, your idea of a good friend was the person who went to the bathroom with you and held your hand as you walked through the scary halls.

In third grade, your idea of a good friend was the person who shared their lunch with you when you forgot yours on the bus.

In sixth grade, your idea of a friend was the person who went up to your new crush, and asked them to dance with you, so that if they said no you wouldn't have to be embarrassed.

In eighth grade, your idea of a good friend was the person who helped you pack up your stuffed animals and old baseball but didn't laugh at you when you finished and broke out in tears.

In eleventh grade, your idea of a good friend was the person who gave you rides in their new car, convinced your parents that you shouldn't be grounded, consoled you when you broke up with your boyfriend, and found you a date to the prom.

At graduation, your idea of a good friend was the person who was crying on the inside but managed the biggest smile one could give as they congratulated you.

The summer after twelfth grade, your idea of a good friend was the person who just silently hugged you as you looked through blurry eyes at 18 years of memories you were leaving behind, and finally on those last days of childhood, went out of their way to give you reassurance that you would make it and sent you off into the world knowing you were loved.

Now, your idea of a good friend is still the person who gives you the better of the two choices, holds your hand when you're scared, helps you fight off those who try to take advantage of you, thinks of you at times when you are not there, reminds you of what you have forgotten, helps you put the past behind you but understands when you need to hold on to it a little longer, stays with you so that you have confidence, goes out of their way to make time for you, helps you clear up your mistakes, helps you deal with pressure from others, smiles for you when they are sad, helps you become a better person, and most importantly, just loves you![3]

Red, White, & Blueberry Parfaits

1 cup of vanilla yogurt or ice cream or vanilla pudding

Fresh or frozen strawberries and blueberries, sweetened with honey

¼ cup crunchy granola cereal

In a tall parfait glass, or bowl, layer vanilla-flavored yogurt, strawberries, more yogurt, blueberries, another layer of yogurt and top with granola.

Refreshing, delicious, and good for big friends and small ones, too!

Part II

▲ ▼ ▲

Two Gals Are
Better Than One

When She's the Other Half
of Your Brain

4

"Verrry Interesting..."

Observant Friends

My sister, Rachel, is the ultimate connoisseur of life's little things. What's amazing about this is that she is married to a man who pays equal attention to detail. This year, when Rach and I arrived at our favorite B&B in Tennessee for our annual sister getaway, she could hardly wait to deliver the detailed Room Report to her husband, Scott. (We both married good men named Scott, but that's pretty much where the similarities in our spouses end.)

As I plopped my tired body across the bed, I couldn't help overhearing Rachel's side of the telephone conversation. "Hi, Honey, we're here at the Rose Garden! Yes...uh-uh. Jim and Shirley, the B&B owners, were dressed in matching black-and-white striped aprons and chef hats when we arrived. Jim had just made a New Orleans bread pudding—hot out of the oven with a warm vanilla hard sauce. Yeah, and they also arranged a delicate bouquet of tea roses in a tiny antique vase for our bedside tables. And this year they've added a white cotton duvet to the bed linens. Oh, what color are the roses? Hmmm...let's see...one is fuchsia with a hint of ecru, another is a delicate peach—no, wait, I think it may have more of an early spring apricot tint around the outermost petals..."

Oh, brother, I thought. *We could be as old as the Delaney sisters by the time she finishes having her say.*

I opted for a relaxing soak in the hot tub while Rachel and her husband regaled each other with the nuances of the upholstery print on the sofa. Thirty minutes later, I strolled in from the hot tub—rested, relaxed, and ready for dinner. To my amazement, Rachel was still doing room detail by phone. To my even greater amazement, her Scott was apparently egging her on, asking question after question, a rapt audience of one.

"The soap is a clear pink glycerin," Rachel was saying, "flat and round, about the size of a diminutive hockey puck. It fits PERFECTLY inside the sea foam green handcrafted pottery dish. I know, I know. It's UNbelievable."

My eye-for-details sister should have been one of those hostesses for the Home Shopping Network—the ones with the amazing ability to talk about a pair of colorless polyester pants in the same sparkling detail as one might describe the Crown Jewels. Or better yet, she could write those incredible wine descriptions for upper-class menus—the ones that make fine vintages sound so marvelous, they read like personal ads: Rich, full-bodied Burgundy with a come-hither hint of playfulness seeks fruity, crisp Chardonnay with subtle, woodsy overtones.

By the time I'd showered, shaved my legs, dressed, and put on my face, Rachel had finally said so long, farewell, auf Wiedersehen, and good-bye to her hubby. I grabbed the receiver (it was still warm from the heat of over-conversing) and dialed my husband's cell phone.

"Hi, Babe!" I singsonged, "we're here! Okay, then, see ya in a couple of days. Love you, too!"

Click.

Done.

"You didn't even tell him about the Pecan Coconut Bohemian Bundt Cake Shirley baked for us!" Rachel exclaimed.

"Trust me," I said, "it's a detail my Scott can live without." Rubbing my grumbling tummy, I added, "I'm starving. Why don't you go lather yourself up with the rose-scented hockey puck and put on your brown suit..."

"Sienna."

"Come again?"

"It's burnt sienna, with a sepia-toned belt."

I looked toward the ceiling and sighed, while my sister flashed a mischievous grin and darted for the bathroom (or should I say, "The comfort closet adorned in a stunning array of floral linens, delicately accented with a roving vine motif...").

This spring, I had several speaking engagements within easy driving distance to Rachel's new Southern-based home of Atlanta. So, she'd hop in the car with me once my plane arrived at the airport, and off we'd go, like Ethel and Lucy, on a road trip together. On every getaway trip, my notable sister gave me pause to think and often laugh aloud. She's like a female Jerry Seinfeld, a master at observing the quirks of life that others miss. And it's one of the things I've loved about having my little sister tag along ever since we were kids.

Last week we drove up together to spend the day at a lodge in North Carolina, set on picturesque Lake Lure and surrounded by the blue-green barrier of the Great Smoky

Mountains. The 1930s lodge was picture-perfect, the grounds surrounding it, a living bouquet of spring flowers and foliage. (Of course Rachel had researched and found this little haven for us ahead of time.) As we went out to take a morning stroll, we happened upon a pair of cement Chinese dragons placed, obviously, as exotic accents to the gardens. But as we got a little closer to the Chinese figurines, Rachel's sharp eye—and sharp wit—caught me off guard.

"Hey, Beck—look at those dragons! They're bucktoothed. Those two could eat bamboo shoots through a picket fence."

Sure enough, upon closer inspection I could see that the dragons each sported an amazing set of Billy Bob uppers. Though I am sure the designer meant them to look ferocious, they looked more like dragon twins who just barely graduated from Oriental Slow Class. Each dragon had about 20 teeth, all the same size, like a row of white Chiclets so big they concealed any evidence of a bottom lip.

I couldn't help laughing. "You know, Rach, you're right. I think that's one of the most impressive overbites I've ever seen on a yard ornament."

At this point, Rachel employed her best hillbilly accent, stuck her front teeth out and took on the persona of the slanty-eyed, toothy twin statues. "Why howdy there, y'all. We're the Bubba Dragons! Come on in and put yer feet up! How 'bout some moo goo gai pan 'n' grits?"

By this time I was laughing so hard I had to sit down on a nearby bench and cross my legs to keep from wetting my pants.

The next morning, while Rachel went out alone on her walk through the Red-Neck Chinese gardens, I packed both of our suitcases and threw them into the car. I had a speaking engagement that evening, and I've learned the hard way that it's best not to let Rachel pack her own luggage when we have a schedule to keep. Her details personality means that while I'm using the wad-'em-up, squish 'em in, sit on it, and zip 'er up method of packing, Rach is folding each pair of her cotton briefs, one pair at a time, into neat little party-sandwich-shaped bundles. It's enough to give me apoplexy.

Thankfully, Rachel tends to be easygoing, so she didn't mind my headin' us up and movin' us out while she meandered through the fauna and flora around the lake's edge. When I delivered the news that we had to get on the road, Rach followed me to the car, where she saw the humor in yet another detail I'd overlooked.

"Beck," she said, a chuckle rising like soft bubbles to the surface of her voice. "Did you see that sign on our rental car?"

I glanced at it and read out loud, "Monitored by passive security system."

"Now what does that mean?" She mused. "Does that mean pacifists are guarding the car? Like if someone tries to steal it, they'll hear a recording say, 'Pretty please we'd like to ask you not to break into this car, for we are peace-loving police and truly wish you no harm. We love you, man. From Your Friendly Neighborhood Passive Security Guards.'"

Again, I had to hurry to assume a cross-legged sitting position so I could laugh with abandon. (Those of you who've had multiple children know what I mean. After giving birth to four children, one has to plan where one can safely sneeze and let go with a belly laugh. We are not in Depends yet, but we can see soggy days on the horizon.)

Eventually we got on the road, arriving at our destination in Georgia. While I busied myself setting up the book table, Rachel mingled with the locals. Within minutes, a lovely

Southern belle came up to me and drawled, "I like your sister. She's real wheeeety."

"She's what?" I asked. Though I'm Southern, I only speak fluent Texan, which is still a couple of states removed from the genteel language of my friends from Mobile and Atlanta.

"She's wheaty," the woman repeated, pronouncing the word exactly the same way, but saying it at a slightly faster clip.

Just then Rachel poked her head from behind the woman's shoulder, like the head of a hand puppet, and translated. "Beck, she thinks I'm witty!"

I smiled and nodded. "That you are."

What more could one ask for than to have a sister/friend who sees fine art in a soap dish, slapstick in yard ornaments, and humor in warning signs?

I have good news for you reader-friends. Rachel has now joined the ranks of women writers in our family tree. And if you've enjoyed the funny stories in my books, just wait until you meet my wheeety sister.

Why, she's more fun than a barrel of buck-toothed dragons.

He who is of a merry heart has a continual feast.
PROVERBS 15:15 NKJV

"Among those whom I like or admire, I can find no common denominator, but among those whom I love, I can: all of them make me laugh."
—W.H. Auden

Becky's Best Girlfriend Hints
for Handling "Details, Details..."

Organization is NOT my strong suit, but here are two systems that ACTUALLY WORK to keep this scatter-brained mom from going completely crazy with the details of managing a large family and a small career.

Paper Tiger Tamer

Buy a small, open (no lid) plastic, portable hanging file holder and set it on the kitchen table or where you usually read and sort mail. (It should hold about 7 to 10 fairly full files, comfortably.)

Label each file with a different family member's name, and also label files for "bills to be paid," "coupons," "receipts," and "stamps 'n' stuff." (This is where I put a checkbook, stamps, envelopes, and paper and pen to make bill paying and letter writing a snap.)

This has been a paper tiger tamer for our crazy family.

Laundry Sorting Simplified

Find a room in your house where you can put a long table (like the ones used for church suppers) against a wall. Underneath the table line up laundry baskets, one for each member in your family. On top of the table, do the very same thing. (I know, that's TWO laundry baskets per family member, but the investment is oh-so-worth-it. And you can find plastic laundry baskets at great prices at discount stores.)

"Underneath-the-table baskets" are where each family can put their dirty clothes in their own labled basket. After these clothes are washed and dried, clean clothes can go in the correct "top-of-the-table basket" to be folded, sorted, and put away at the family member's whim and schedule.

A life-simplifying tip: Train your kids early to do their own laundry. Mine started about age 8 or 9, and once they figured it out, they *hated* anyone else doing their laundry because "Nobody does it right!" Nobody gets the blame for turning brother's shorts pink or shrinking mom's best sweater. Everybody is responsible for their *own* clothes.

If you want, you can also label one set of baskets "Miscellaneous" and have the kids put their sheets and towels in this one.

Layered Mexican Dip

(This is a great recipe for those observant friends who will enjoy viewing and figuring out the many layers of this easy, always-a-hit party dip)

2 cans refried beans (the flavored ones are best)
1 carton sour cream
1 carton avocado dip or ½ c. guacamole
1 ½ c. picante sauce
2 c. grated cheese
½ cup green onions, chopped
1 small can black olives, sliced and drained
1 tomato, chopped

Layer ingredients in the order given in a large, clear, oblong Pyrex dish. Serve with tortilla chips or Fritos or soft, warmed flour or corn tortillas.

5

"No Problem..."

Can-Do Friends

My parents dropped by for a visit. I had planned on making sandwiches for lunch but I had one small problem. I could not for the life of me find the brand new loaf of bread I'd had out on the counter just an hour before.

"Well, Becky," Mother said after we looked in all the usual places bread might hide, "we used to find just about everything that was missing under your bed when you were a teenager at home. Have you checked there?"

"Mother, I really don't think..." I started to protest, but decided to check anyway. I'd been on five weeks of pain medication after my bicycle "sports injury," and my brain was more fried, rather than its normal state of scrambled. So who was to say that I might not have tucked it under the bed? But a quick under-the-bed search yielded nothing but a rotting banana peel and an old tennis shoe, and though we were starving and desperate by then, I decided neither the peel nor the shoe could be used to make a decent sandwich.

"Checked the bathroom yet?" my father asked, and I knew right then that my folks are probably the only parents in the world who could ask their daughter, with straight faces, if she might have stored a loaf of bread in the bathroom. What could I do but dutifully check all the bathroom cabinets—but alas, nary a shred of wheat turned up.

The Hunt for the Loaf of Wonder went on for about 15 more minutes—as we searched the freezer, the TV cabinet, the trunk of my car, and my home office. Still no dough.

At this point, my personal assistant and office manager, Rose Dodson, breezed in the front door and paused by the kitchen to say hello to my folks.

"Rose," my mother half-whispered in a just-between-us-girls sort of way. "Becky seems to have misplaced an *entire* loaf of bread. You work with her nearly every day; would you happen to have any idea where she might have put it?"

"Did you try the microwave?" Rose asked without blinking an eye.

"Why would I put it in the micro...?" I started to ask, but was interrupted by the sound of the microwave door opening and euphoric shouts of "Eureka!"

"Rose, you are a genius!" my mother exclaimed. "How did you know?"

"I just tried to think of what I would do if I were Becky and got distracted."

"Amazing," my mother said.

"Astounding," my father agreed.

Rose just nodded and said, "Just doin' my job, that's all—doin' my job."

Rose is, indeed, a rare flower among the garden of my female friends. Never in my life have I met a person with such Can Do in their mental shoes.

Rose's appearance is somewhat of a contradiction. Let me explain. When Rose accompanies me anywhere, the first thing everyone notices is her cameo beauty. She walks into a room, and people look up and think someone escaped from a countryside scene in a Victorian film. Her face is delicate, with porcelain skin; her smile, like a perfect pink rose bud, and her eyes, a stunning blue. But it's her hair that crowns her glory; it cascades in the most beautiful dark golden spirals and ringlets around her face and down her back. Her favorite styles are long dresses or skirts in pretty country prints. She's a caring mother of four, and loving wife of one Fred. She cooks and sews, and loves gardens and grandmas and God. She never attended college, choosing children over career for almost all of her young life. At first glance, one might assume she's as delicate as a flower petal.

One would have assumed wrong. Trust me—there's lots of metal in those petals.

Need someone to partner or belay you on a rock climb? Rose is your handy-dandy Spiderwoman.

Need a co-captain to steer your sailing vessel? Rose has sailed the seas for weeks at a time with Fred and their cargo of kids.

Your car won't start? Let her check under the hood—nine times out of ten she can diagnose the problem within minutes.

Need furniture assembled or a computer put together or wood trimming put up on your living room walls? Just yelp, "Rose, help!" and hand her the hammer.

When her daughter, Hope, wanted to be legally adopted and take Fred's last name (so she wouldn't feel different from her step-brother and sisters), did Rose hire a lawyer? No, sir. Move over, Erin Brockavich: Rose researched, completed, and filed a three-inch stack of papers with the court.

Then representing herself and her family, she transformed Hope into a legalized Dodson.

Stretching their modest budget taut, Rose managed to purchase and rent out two homes besides the one that she and Fred live in. She knows how to play the stock market with the best of Wall Street Internet wizards. She can make sense out of the flowery hat boxes I stuff with receipts each week—and pencil-whip a tax form well enough to knock H&R off their block.

She organized a two-day-a-week program for an entire town of homeschoolers, as well as homeschooled her own brood until just a few years ago. She's survived the ultimate test of interior female fortitude: she substitute-taught in her childrens' public school and served on the local PTA.

She is not just a receptionist—she's a Guard Secretary, shielding me from more than I can possibly handle and treating my career as OUR business—which it is, because without Rose I'd have to quit and go straight to the insane asylum. Woe to the telephone company who charges us more than they should. Pity on the person who tries to best her at negotiation.

Sometimes she acts as my stand-in, a "Mini Me," if you will. For example, if I'm called upon to speak locally and cannot because of a too-tight schedule, Rose pipes up with a cheerful, "Now, did you know that I speak to church groups as well? I'll bring Becky's books and tell stories on her and tell you my own stories and we'll all have a great time. It'll be almost like having Becky there!" The first time she ventured out to speak to a local group, though she fought down her share of nerves, she received a rousing standing ovation—from the audience and from Fred and the kids who were proudly waiting outside of the auditorium.

This past spring, I asked Rose to accompany me to a large speaking engagement, and before I even got to the hotel, she'd decorated and set up the book table, charmed and reassured the event planners, and stocked the hotel fridge with healthy goodies. Whenever Rose was at the book table, we sold twice as many books. She worked the table like a true saleswoman, chatting it up with moms standing in line, stuffing a Kleenex into a copy of *Real Magnolias* and describing it to women as "a chick flick in a book." (Rose's own incredible story—of being abandoned by her minister husband after giving birth to her daughter—and her miraculous marriage to Fred, the single father of three young children, is in *Real Magnolias*.) Who could resist such Southern-style marketing?

When she first began working for me, Rose took my "office" of skewed pictures, half-eaten apples, boxes of books, and at least a dozen Tupperware containers of papers—all marked "miscellaneous"—and while I was gone on a long weekend, turned it into a smooth operation that even I can understand.

When we went through several frustrating experiences with professional Web site designers in an effort to launch a high quality Web site to our liking, Rose called me on my cell phone one day and in exasperation announced, "Becky, I've had it. While you're out and about, get me a book on Web site designing. I'm going to learn how to do this myself. It can't be that hard."

Though several computer programmers warned me that Web site building wasn't for amateurs, all I could tell them was, "Look, you don't understand. We're dealing with a Rose, here."

Rose stayed up two nights reading *Building a Web Site for Dummies* and proved that she was certainly no dummy. Our colorful, complicated site (www.beckyfreeman.com) is a virtual picture that says more than I could describe in a thousand words. As soon as she had our Web pages in place, she figured out how to take credit cards on-line to streamline our author-signed, mail-order book business. When I complained of standing in line at the post office to mail orders, she quickly connected us to a Web site that prints postage in the comfort of our little office.

Just before I asked Rose if she would come work with me, she went with me to a writers' conference where I was speaking. Completely inspired by the weekend, she said, with eyes sparkling, "Someday I'm going to be a *great* writer." What impressed me then and impresses me still, is that she didn't say, "Gee I'd like to write and publish something someday." Instead, with whole-hearted conviction she stated *out loud* that she would be a GREAT writer. That was a couple of years ago. I'm now reading Rose's first book proposal, and you know what? I think she's going to make it to the great writer mark—and I'll be the first one standing in line when her future best-seller hits the bookstores.

(I showed the above list of Rose's virtues to my editing buddy, Gracie, and she wrote back to say, "This is good, but don't you think you ought to leave SOMEthing for Rose's eulogy someday?" Rose and I both enjoyed a good laugh, and then, ironically, Rose ended up having a week filled with one mistake or mishap after another. We decided it was God's way of keeping her humble.)

Typically, Rose comes in around 9:00 A.M. and catches me in my pajamas, no make-up, hair going every which way like a startled goose—e-mailing family, friends, and fans. (I confess: I'm a little addicted to e-mail. It's so much fun to read!) Then we mosey to the kitchen for coffee talk and, depending on the amount of drama in the ongoing soap operas of our lives, we spend some time visiting. Some days there have been tears in our mugs, accompanied by heartfelt prayers. Other days we are in Real Businesswomen Mode and quickly jot down a list of important to-do's for the day. But we both confess to feeling like two little girls playing "office" most days. How could work be this much fun?

Sometime around noon, I usually make us some lunch—sometimes we take a break to eat at the kitchen table; sometimes we munch sandwiches at separate computers.

One afternoon, over a kitchen-table lunch, I asked Rose a question I'd always wanted to ask.

"Rose, what in the world gave you that deep-seated conviction that you could tackle just about anything life threw at you? How did you become such a Jill of All Trades?"

"You know, I think part of it was the resilience I had to learn from a tough growing-up period," Rose explained thoughtfully, as she picked up a chip and dipped it in salsa. "My mother and father divorced, and for some time me and my sisters were left in the care of my grandmother. My father later married a kind-hearted woman and took us home to live with them. Dad, though he made mistakes, began to fix what had been broken in our lives. He started going to church and infusing us girls with the knowledge that anything could be overcome. Anything could be fixed—with a little faith, some creative thinking, a few trips to the library for research, and a lot of hard work."

A few days later, I met Rose and Fred, along with her father and stepmother, at a local café for a Saturday morning bacon and eggs breakfast. I asked her dad, point blank, what had caused Rose to be so positive, so willing to learn new things. "Becky, I don't know for sure, but I always knew that if you loved your kids and trusted them—even at a young age—they could exceed typical expectations. I let my

girls do things like climb trees and saw off branches, drive
the farm tractors, and work on equipment, explaining the
how-to's the best I could and then just letting them go to
figure out the rest by practicing."

I turned toward Dorothy, Rose's stepmom—whom Rose
simply refers to as "Mom." "When Rose came to live with
you, was she a confident child?"

"Oh, no, she was so tiny and scared. Scared of me, too,
I'm sure. Aren't all stepmothers supposed to be wicked, after
all? But I'd set her up on the counter and hand her a bowl,
and together we'd whip up a batch of sugar cookies and
talk and talk. After loving her and encouraging her to try
new things, she just blossomed—opened up like a flower."

At this point, Dorothy wiped at a tear in her eye, her
voice breaking. "When my own mother was sick and dying,
no one but little Rose could comfort her. Here was this small
child, this young girl, spooning food into a sick old woman's
mouth—when no one else in the family had been able to get
Grandma to eat. Rose was just a wonder with her. It meant
the world to me that my little stepdaughter had such compassion with my mother—and that my mother loved her so
much as well."

Rose smiled shyly—perhaps the first time I'd seen that
sort of little-girl smile on my competent girlfriend's face—
and I saw just a glimpse of the child she once was.

In that smoky, small town café, I sipped strong coffee
and listened to the deep Southern accents recounting stories
of a family once lost, now found again. Rose grew up determined to let bygones be bygones, so that when her birth
mother—who'd never really been the sort of mother a young
girl needs—called Rose to say she was dying of cancer, Rose
went and ministered love to her, allowing her mother the
privilege of expressing her sorrow and remorse and of

leaving this life in peace. Rose told me that she was greatly influenced at an early age by the words of Betsey ten Boom, sister to Corrie ten Boom. Under the cruelty of the Nazis, Corrie struggled with a deep-seated rage, but Betsey's words to her were, "No hate, Corrie. No hate."

"I think this became my motto for all that went wrong in my life," Rose continued: "Being one of the 'poor-little-girls-from-the-divorced-family'; the absence of my real mother; my first husband abandoning me and our newborn daughter for another woman. At each point, I knew I had two choices—to let the hate burn a hole in my heart or let go, forgive, and let God's love keep flowing."

I thought of Rose's words all that Saturday afternoon.

And I realized that struggle can be one of the greatest gifts God gives His children. It's been said roots grow deepest in places where storms blow the hardest. Rose's roots are deep and sure because of the storms she's survived. God has brought her this far and she knows He'll take her on home. Having overcome so much in her life, she has an uncanny sense of assurance from God, one I wish for my children and myself—the assurance that she and God can face whatever life hands them, whether it's a major trauma like illness or death, or the small daily dramas like a computer glitch that's giving us fits or a carburetor that sticks.

The other day, Rose brought her 12-year-old daughter, Hope, along while she worked. On such occasions, Hope usually watches a video or does some small "office work" for us—addressing envelopes or stamping mail. On this occasion, Hope got hungry, and Rose told her to go make herself a sandwich.

"Mom!" she called from the kitchen to the office where Rose was typing on the computer. "I can't find the mayonnaise. I don't want to make this sandwich myself. Can you come make it?"

I called to Rose from where I was standing in the dining room just a few feet from Hope. "Don't worry; I'll help her!"

"No! Wait!" Rose called back to me. I stopped in my tracks. Rose got up out of her chair, moved toward us, looked calmly and sternly at Hope, and with only a hint of a smile said, "Hope, it's just a sandwich. I'm not asking you to build a cathedral here. You can do this without our help. If you can't find what you need, use something else. You are quite capable of making your own lunch."

Hope nodded, and soon I heard her humming quietly while assembling a very respectable sandwich. All by herself, without any help.

A little Can-do Rosebud in the making.

I know what it is to be in need, and I know what it is to have plenty. I have learned the secret of being content in any and every situation, whether well fed or hungry, whether living in plenty or in want. I can do everything through him who gives me strength.
PHILIPPIANS 4:12,13

"Pain nourishes courage.
You can't be brave if you've only had
wonderful things happen to you."
—Mary Tyler Moore, *Women Say the Wisest Things*

Can-Do Girlfriend Test of Courage:
Are You Brave Enough to Be a Parent Yet?

MESS TEST
Smear peanut butter on the sofa and curtains. Place a fish stick behind the couch and leave it there all summer.

TOY TEST
Obtain a 55-gallon box of Legos (or you may substitute roofing tacks). Have a friend spread them all over the house. Put on a blindfold. Try to walk to the bathroom or kitchen. Do not scream because this would wake a child at night.

GROCERY STORE TEST
Borrow one or two small animals (goats are best) and take them with you as you shop. Always keep them in sight and pay for anything they eat or damage.

DRESSING TEST
Obtain one large, unhappy, live octopus. Stuff into a small net bag making sure that all the arms stay inside.

FEEDING TEST
Obtain a large plastic milk jug. Fill halfway with water. Suspend from the ceiling with a cord. Start the jug swinging. Try to insert spoonfuls of soggy cereal into the mouth of the jug, while pretending to be an airplane. Now dump the contents of the jug on the floor.

NIGHT TEST
Prepare by obtaining a small cloth bag and filling it with 8 to 12 pounds of sand. Soak it thoroughly in water. At 3:00 P.M.

begin to waltz and hum with the bag until 9:00 P.M. Lay down your bag and set your alarm for 10:00 P.M. Get up, pick up your bag, and sing every song you have ever heard. Make up about a dozen more and sing these, too, until 4:00 A.M. Set alarm for 5:00 A.M. Get up and make breakfast. Keep this up for five years. Look cheerful.

INGENUITY TEST

Take an egg carton. Using a pair of scissors and pot of paint, turn it into an alligator. Now take a toilet paper tube and turn it into an attractive Christmas candle. Use only Scotch tape and a piece of foil. Lastly, take a milk carton, a ping-pong ball, and an empty box of Cocoa Puffs. Make an exact replica of the Eiffel Tower.

AUTOMOBILE TEST

Forget the BMW and buy a station wagon. Buy a chocolate ice cream cone and put it in the glove compartment. Leave it there. Get a dime. Stick it into the cassette player. Take a family-size package of chocolate chip cookies. Mash them into the back seat. Run a garden rake along both sides of the car. There, perfect.

PHYSICAL TEST (Women)

Obtain a large beanbag chair and attach it to the front of your clothes. Leave it there for nine months. Now remove ten of the beans. And try not to notice your closet full of clothes. You won't be wearing them for a while.

PHYSICAL TEST (Men)

Go to the nearest drugstore. Set your wallet on the counter. Ask the clerk to help himself. Now proceed to the nearest food store. Go to the head office and arrange for your paycheck to be directly deposited to the store. Purchase a newspaper. Go home and read it quietly for the last time.

FINAL ASSIGNMENT

Find a couple who already have a small child. Lecture them on how they can improve their discipline, patience, tolerance, toilet training, and the child's table manners. Suggest many ways they can improve. Emphasize to them that they should never allow their children to run wild. Enjoy this experience. It will be the last time you will have all the answers.[4]

"I Can DO it MYSELF!"

Becky's Quick MYOB (Make Your Own Breakfast) Ideas

Because I'm not a morning person at all, I encourage my children (and husband) to cook their own quick, easy nutritious breakfasts. (With the way I cook in the morning, this didn't take much encouraging.)

There's the ever popular "cereal with milk." (Scott and I love Shredded Wheat with honey and milk. He grew up eating this and I thought it was the oddest thing—until I tried it. It's wonderful!) But here's a couple more quick, yummy breakfasts the family enjoys. (And makes themselves!)

Hot Fruit 'n' Oatmeal (good for kids who don't like their oatmeal too slimy!)

Chop up a piece of fruit in a microwavable bowl. (Apple, peach, pear, mango, banana, etc.)

Sprinkle it with a little brown sugar (1 T.) a dab of butter (1 t.). (A few miniature marshmallows are yummy too, making a nice thick "sauce" as they melt.) Cover all this with about 3 heaping tablespoons of raw, old-fashioned oatmeal.

Cover the bowl with a small plate and microwave for about 3 minutes.

Serve with a little milk or cream. (Or for an afternoon dessert, top with ice cream!)

Eggs in a Bowl

Break two eggs into a microwavable bowl that has been sprayed with Pam. Top with a plate. Microwave 1-2 minutes until eggs are set the way you like them. Sprinkle with salt and pepper and enjoy! Quick and no added fat.

Extra hint: when you don't have time to boil eggs for tuna or egg-salad sandwiches, this is a great way to get eggs cooked for your dish in no time!

Brown Sugar 'n' Cinnamon Toast

If you've never made cinnamon toast with real butter and brown sugar (with or without cinnamon)—instead of white sugar and cinnamon—you are in for a wonderful treat. Try it!

Fruit Slush

Peel slightly over-ripe bananas and freeze them in a Ziploc bag for the kids to use to make their own fruit slushies. Just put 1 frozen banana, 1 c. milk or favorite juice, and any other fruit (frozen, fresh, or canned) that hits your fancy into a blender and blend well. Add a few ice cubes if you want a thicker drink. Makes 1-2 servings.

Peanut Butter 'n' Honey Toast

In my family of origin, our favorite breakfast treat was to mix up a couple of spoonfuls of peanut butter with honey or maple syrup then spread it on hot buttered toast. I still love this treat. Especially good with toasted healthy nutty bread, natural peanut butter, and pure maple syrup (the kind that comes from real trees, no sugar added). Ezekiel Bread (at health food stores) is my favorite.

Part III

▲ ▼ ▲

Bring Out the Pom-Poms!

Cheering Each Other
Through Terror and Triumph

6

"What Have We Got to Lose?"

Entrepreneurial Friends

I call it the year I impersonated an agent.

Not a secret agent, a la *Mission Impossible*. But a literary agent. (On second thought, it might have been closer to *Mission Impossible* than I realized at the time.)

It all began innocently enough. I was having my every-six-months lunch date at La Madeline's with Tina Jacobsen. We always order the same thing: Chicken Caesar Salad, Tomato Basil Soup, Strawberries Romanoff, and lots of French Coffee with good thick cream. We always talk about the same thing: How excited we both are about the 47 different new projects we've just taken on, and how crazy we are to have gotten ourselves so busy and exhausted from—you guessed it—tackling 47 new projects all at once. This conversation has changed very little in the last seven years, so we're thinking we must be gluttons for creativity overload.

Tina is one of those women that absolutely amazes me. She's so laid back and casual and comfortable to be around, a dark-haired Helen Hunt type with long legs that wind around chair legs and crisscross on sofa cushions like limp fettuccini. She's as at home entertaining friends in sweats, surrounded by kids and boxes of cereal on a Saturday morning as she is in an all-business suit, negotiating with clients on Monday. Tina runs a terrific public relations firm, Books and Bookings Media, in a large (but still cozy) two-story-house-turned-office-building in the small town of Corsicana, Texas. Which is also famous for its fruitcakes. Not that this has anything to do with Tina, mind you.

Tina has several employees, a full-time on-site day care, and dozens of high-profile clients. I am constantly dropping my jaw at the things Tina will tackle with a "why not try it?" attitude. Just hanging around women like her fills my courage tank with confidence gas. (You know, I have a feeling my editor is going to make me change the metaphors in the previous sentence. But it's late and my creativity is lagging, so I'm going to leave it as is, and we'll see if I can get away with it.)

The first time I met Tina was by phone. She'd been hired to do the radio publicity for my first book. One hot summer afternoon she called and said, "Hi Becky, you ready for your first interview for *Worms in My*...ooops! My five-year-old daughter just tossed her shoe off her foot and hit herself in the head. Be back with you in a sec...."

I knew from that first sentence out of Tina's mouth that we were going to be friends. She laughed when I later called to report on my first-ever phone radio interview. (Little did I dream back then that I would do over 400 of them within a few short years!) "Tina," I said, "I think I did pretty well in spite of the kids' letting Daisy and Colonel run barking through the house, and Gabe's holding up a rattlesnake he'd just killed in the middle of the interview. Thankfully, I was talking about being a mom in the country with critter-loving kids so I think all the interruptions added a hint of authenticity."

Since that first encounter with Tina, there have been many more—mostly lunch—dates near Dallas malls, but we've also been on a couple of business trips together. And in spite of my losing my purse in an airport bathroom on one such occasion, she's remained my very good friend. Today I do voice work for two of B&B Media's radio shows: *The Little Bookshop* and *Secret Place Devotions.* In exchange for my recordings, Tina helps advertise my Web site. It's the way women do business—we switch out, trade, help each other, and network in web-like fashion. (Men seem to prefer the less messy, but less fun, pyramid chain-of-command in business.) As Faith Popcorn, trend-predictor and business consultant, says in her newest book about marketing to women, "Women cross-pollinate. They take the powdery-fine residue from one story and dust it on the next...women naturally reinforce their bond by freely and clearly dispensing information, directions or heartfelt help."[5]

Tina's entrepreneurial savvy has always been an inspiration to me, and I suppose that's why that spring day at La Madeleine's, I nonchalantly answered, "Why not?" to her question, "How'd you like to be a literary agent and work under the umbrella of my company's name?"

After all, what did we have to lose?

How hard could it be to be a literary agent, anyway?

I had a bunch of friends back in Greenville and Dallas, and they all said they wanted to write a book. I'd been a first grade teacher and knew how to put together a portfolio for my class of students. I knew a few editors from my own publishing experience. Okay, so I knew *two* editors. Still, I was convinced that all I had to do was put two and two together and—voila!—out would come a bunch of published authors and we'd net 15 percent of their royalties.

So this is how I found myself, three months later dressed in a bright blue power suit, pulling a suitcase full of my friends' manuscripts down the aisles of the Christian Booksellers Association Convention (CBA). Nobody told me what a naïve and gutsy thing it was for an author, new to this business herself, to call herself a literary agent. No one told me how ludicrous it was to try to sell manuscripts to senior editors at major publishers on behalf of friends, many of whom had never even published an article, much less a book.

And since nobody thought to tell me it couldn't be done, and Tina obviously believed in me, I just did it. Never asked another agent for advice. Never looked up *How to Be a Literary Agent* at the library. I just made a business card that said "Becky Freeman, Literary Agent" and from there kind of guessed my way around the job and tried to think like an editor. And here's what I thought: If I were an editor, I would be tired of reading lots of little words on thick stacks of paper. All I'd want to see, at first glance, is a great title with a good visual hook, and maybe some pictures, photos, and cover art possibilities. I'd want the book summed up in one phrase, then one sentence, and if that intrigued me, I'd be willing to scan a paragraph. I'd want to read a one- or two-page easy-to-read outline with lots of white space and organized sections with headings in bold print. And I'd want to have an appointment set before the convention, where the agent made every minute count—pitching proposals in a short amount of time the way screenwriters pitch movie ideas to Hollywood producers.

So I visited with each of my wannabe authors/friends/ clients and shared my vision. I honed down their proposals, helped them with titles, and asked them for something fun, colorful, and flat that I could use as a visual aid for their projects. If my clients' proposals got published, we'd have lots of wins to celebrate: They'd get advances and the honor of calling themselves authors, and I'd get to make a little profit from their success. But best of all, I'd get a whole collection of girlfriends with whom I could talk about writing. So, I made deep-breath phone calls and lined up a week of appointments at the convention with eight editors at eight different publishing houses.

When I saw two well-known agents walking down the hall at the convention, looking like Executive Ken dolls from *GQ Twins* magazine, for the first time since my enthusiastic start out of the agenting shoot, I got nervous. I couldn't help notice that the sharply dressed duo each carried one neat leather briefcase. I was hauling around a small travel suitcase on wheels. One of my kids had wound an orange pipe cleaner around the handle in order to attach a couple of jingle bells to it. (Do not ask me why he did this. Does anyone know why children do half of the creative little things children do?) I could not, for the life of me, unwind the pipe cleaner, so I resigned myself to ding-a-linging with every click of my high-heeled shoes.

Peeking around a corner, straining for a glimpse of Real Agents at Work, I observed them opening up linen folders gold-embossed with their company logo and filled with professional proposals: thick slabs of pristine white paper covered with uniformly typed black words.

It was then that it dawned on me that there might actually be an established "system" for agents presenting proposals to editors.

I suddenly felt like Elly Mae Clampett, Literary Agent from Yahoo County. Or like little Loretta Lynn when she arrived on the doorstep of the Grand Ol' Opry from the hills of Kentucky with nothing but her geetar, a homemade dress, and a good-hearted man named Doo. (What I would have given for a good-hearted Doo right then who would hold my hand and assure me I wouldn't throw up when I sang my pitch and showed wares to the nice editor people.)

I sat down on a bench outside a convention door and unzipped my suitcase, which felt strangely like a hobo's knapsack at this point. I was afraid someone might offer me a sandwich or some change. Reaching inside the suitcase, I pulled out an enormous black vinyl binder filled with book proposals arranged Becky Style. In other words, my clients— these dear unsuspecting friends who had trusted me to represent their work—had given me their manuscripts, and I'd managed to arrange them exactly as one might expect an Early Childhood Educator would.

Next to Ellie Kay's *Shop, Save, and Share* proposal, I had tucked in a picture of Ellie wearing a slightly askew crown and written underneath it: "Ellie Kay, The Coupon Queen." I'd also stapled one of Ellie's grocery receipts where she saved a typical 60 percent on her week's worth of groceries and surrounded that by stickers of bananas and apples and tiny grocery sacks.

Next to Brenda Waggoner's proposal for *The Velveteen Woman*, I'd put stickers of soft stuffed bunnies and then stamped bunny footprints around her photo and professional counselor business card.

Kali Schneider had found some beautiful stickers of chocolate truffles that I used to spruce up her *Truffles from Heaven* manuscript.

Jane Jarrell, a Christian Martha Stewart (with a sense of humor and a husband who likes her) gave me bright, colorful proposals with cover sheets that looked like wrapped packages along with magazine photos of her food-styling handiwork.

Annette Smith was a storyteller extraordinaire—the sort that could make you laugh in one sentence and tear up in the next, and so I had color highlighted the best paragraph in her *Whispers of Angels* manuscript and dubbed her a "female Robert Fulghum."

And on the list went. The more I stared at the hodge-podge notebook of colorful pictures and photos, tucked between short (albeit well-written) proposals, the more I wanted to run out the door before somebody discovered I was an imposter and arrested me before I could plead insanity.

But I'd gone too far to back out now. My friends were counting on me. Tina had put her company's name behind what I would represent. And an editor was calling my name.

"Becky, are you ready for our appointment?"

"No," I wanted to say. "But do you happen to have any spare medication?"

Instead I put on my brightest smile to cover my deepest fear—rejection—and walked into the publisher's booth, toting my suitcase full of construction-paper-and-paste proposals behind me.

Only God and His mercy and His great sense of humor could deliver me now.

> *When I am afraid, I will trust in you....*
> *What can mortal man do to me?*
> PSALM 56:3,4

"Courage is fear
that has said its prayers."
—DOROTHY BERNARD

Girlfriend to Girlfriend Fear Busters

Whenever I need to gather my courage about me to do something out of my comfort zone (which has been incredibly often these past few years), I re-read the classic book on conquering fear by Susan Jeffers called *Feel the Fear and Do It Anyway.*[6] Here are some quotes from this little book that help me whenever I feel afraid (and holding my head erect and whistling a happy tune isn't doing the trick).

You Are NOT Alone:
"Not only am I going to experience fear whenever I'm on unfamiliar territory, but so is everyone else."

Consider the Alternative:
"Pushing through fear is less frightening than living with the underlying fear that comes from a feeling of helplessness."

Real Growth Involves Facing Fear:
"The fear will never go completely away as long as you continue to grow."

(In other words, if you aren't doing something that scares you just a little bit, you may not be stretching and growing.)

"Ships in harbor are safe,
but that's not what ships are built for."
—John Shedd

Get You a Group of Cheerleaders
"It is amazingly empowering to have the support of a strong, motivated and inspirational group of people."

As believers in the Most High God, we possess the most amazing fear-buster—the realization that He wants to work through you and me. I'm His vessel—this is why I'm on earth. You're His vessel—you have a purpose larger than yourself.

All we have to do is allow Him to teach, guide, open doors and hearts, and use us.

Remember, "There is no fear in love" (1 John 4:18 NKJV). In fact, I believe the opposite of love IS fear (not hate). Focus on letting God's love flow through, and fear will melt away. (Eventually...I promise.)

Wow 'Em Strawberry/Pretzel Dish

(A Fruit Salad, but Yummy Enough to Be Dessert. Make this when you want to impress your friends at work, at church, or at a party. People will hunt you down for the recipe!)

2 c. crushed pretzels

3 T. sugar

¾ c. butter, melted

8 oz. cream cheese

2 c. Cool Whip

1 6 oz. package strawberry Jell-O

2 cups frozen strawberries (unsweetend)

Mix pretzels, 3 T. sugar, and butter together and press into a 9 x 13 inch greased pan. Bake at 400 degrees for 6 minutes. Don't let pretzels burn. Cool, then mix softened cream cheese, and Cool Whip. Spread over pretzel crust. Mix Jell-O with 2 c. boiling water. Cool. Add frozen strawberries and chill until syrupy. Pour over cream cheese layer and chill until ready to serve.

7

"You GO, Girl!"

AttaGirl Friends

I once read with intense fascination that Cary Grant, a boy born into poverty whose real name was Archie Leach, took on the persona of a suave, debonair actor solely by imitation. Skilled at acting from an early age, he could mimic the expressions and movements of almost anyone. In 1920, while crossing the Atlantic with a troupe of performers to New York on the SS *Olympic,* he met Douglas Fairbanks. It was a chance meeting with a man who was to Archie's mind not only tanned and fit but elegant and stylish—what you might call a real gentleman. Cary literally adopted Fairbanks as a role model for what would come to be his own trademark style of laid-back grace and charm.

So if a guy named ARCHIE LEACH could transform himself into Cary Grant, I told myself as I followed the editor to a cubicle in the back of the rented convention room, *then a mother from the country could transform herself into business tycoon and professional agent, Becky Freeman.* Now that I'd seen a few real agents in action that morning, all I had to do was act "as if" I were one of the boys. I held my head up high, walked with confidence, and did my best to ignore the ding-ding-a-linging of the pipe cleaner bells on my suitcase.

Here's where the first miracle began to unfold. The editor actually BELIEVED my act, treating me as if I'd just got off a plane from New York representing John Grisham. (Well maybe that's a bit of an exaggeration, but he didn't throw any tomatoes at me either.) By the time he'd looked over my portfolio and complimented its originality, I was flyin' high. It took all the Cary Grant suave I could mimic to keep from giggling like a schoolgirl when he asked me to send him five of the proposals I was representing. When our time came to an end, I shook his hand and walked away from that meeting room with the confident stride of someone with people to see, places to go, deals to make. Then I darted into the first bathroom I could find, took refuge in a stall and, in Sally Field's famous words, squealed, "They like me! They really LIKE ME!"

On I strolled from appointment to appointment, all day long, gaining new confidence after each meeting, fairly floating on the cloud of my new, emerging businesswoman persona. Somewhere around midday, I decided that my jingle bell briefcase on wheels was probably the very thing that made me stand apart from the rest of the "suits," and ding-a-linged my way through the rest of the week with unconscious pride.

Within a year from that day, I was faced with a set of miraculous victories and one of the most difficult decisions I'd ever have to make.

First, the victories. Almost all of my clients ended up with book contracts that year and today are on their second and third books, most of them making the move from day jobs to writing and speaking full-time. All of their first books did extremely well in the marketplace.

Ellie Kay's *Shop, Save & Share* hit best-seller status and spawned video series, a regular radio spot, and a high-volume Web site!

Brenda's Waggoner's *The Velveteen Woman* was a reader choice in an issue of *Today's Christian Woman* and consistently hovers in the top 10 percent of Amazon.com's book sales.

Annette's first book, *Whispers of Angels,* sold three times what a first-time author usually would sell, receiving wonderful reviews.

Kali, a former top saleswoman in three *Fortune 500* companies, has also created her own signature *Truffles from Heaven* chocolate truffles and a knock-your-socks-off Web site. There's even a beautiful heart-shaped truffle pin available now.

Jane Jarrell is fast on her way to becoming the next Home Living guru—producing a line of beautiful, practical books such as *Love You Can Touch* with her fun, informative engaging style.

The difficult decision: I had a choice to make that was agonizing for me. Though I loved the front-end of agenting (editing, shaping, and selling proposals and mixing it up with authors and editors), the back-end of agenting—negotiations, contracts, phone calls, paperwork, and follow-up—was sapping every available ounce of energy from my own writing and speaking. Too many good things to choose from, and something had to go. I could continue to write my own books and speak or give that up and go into agenting full-time. I just didn't feel I was finished with my own writing career yet (will I ever run out of stories I want to tell?). Thus began the transition from agent to AttaGirl.

I gathered my client friends together and told them that I could no longer agent them but that I'd recommend them to a good friend of mine, an editor recently turned agent. They were disappointed, and I was, too—we'd not only bonded client-to-agent, but friend-to-friend both individually and collectively. Over our months together, we'd enjoyed each other's company as we all met together for lunch at the Cheesecake Factory or Mary of Puddin' Hill or shared suites at the booksellers' convention. Another group of us writing friends from Greenville, calling ourselves The Hens with Pens (me, Gracie Malone, Fran Sandin, Rebecca Jordan, and Suzie Duke) had penned two story collections of our own during this time as well. The first one, *Courage for the Chicken Hearted,* to our delight and surprise, became a best-seller. So, to my former clients we added the happy clucking of the hen friends and began calling the whole kit and caboodle of us "The AttaGirls." Without any real planning or foresight from us, what God had been orchestrating was perhaps one of the greatest Girlfriend Gigs of all time.

For from that humble day when, with great fear and trembling, I shopped my writing wares down the Atlanta Convention Center aisles, has emerged a connected group of women writers who encourage each other, network for each other, pray and celebrate and e-mail and weep and agonize and brainstorm and edit and talk and eat chocolate and laugh and share and—whew!—love each other as sisters in ways that blow my mind some days. We call ourselves The AttaGirls. We've since added writers Lindsey O'Conner, Cheri Fuller, Lynn Morrissey, my sister, Rachel, the "Hens," and several others as our informal network of friendship has grown.

Friendship also crosses over into our individual careers as we AttaGirl each other into whatever spotlight God has given us when He opens a door. For example, when James Robison's *LIFE Today* asked Ellie Kay to write and produce a video series based on her Shop, Save & Share seminars, she wrote many of us AttaGirls into the script. Lindsey and I acted as emcees to a fashion show, where bargain outfits were modeled by none other than several of the AttaGirls. Jane did a segment on the show demonstrating how to make wonderful gifts inexpensively. Kali and Ellie both sported their tiaras: Kali's from winning a beauty contest way back when, Ellie's a vintage antique bargain that she bought to crown herself Coupon Queen. It was a ton of fun and one of the most popular shows *LIFE Today* has aired.

(An aside: at one point in the video production, Ellie was telling a story about a little lady with a heavy New York accent who is supposed to yell, "Ya gonna end up in the POORHOUSE, that's where!" But after two days of non-stop taping, Ellie was more than a little mentally fatigued. She brought the house down when she looked into the camera and accidentally said, "Ya gonna end up in the WHOREHOUSE, that's where!" At which point, in the midst of much falling off of chairs from laughing, she looked at the director and said, deadpan, "I suppose you are going to want a retake of that line, huh?" Stories like these that we can tell on each other only add to the crazy glue that bonds us together forever.)

As we continue to write, and our friendships continue to blossom, more and more of our books are sprinkled with tributes and thanks and stories told on each other. Flowers with notes arrive, signed, "Love, The AttaGirls" on doorsteps of those of us suffering an illness or loss, or celebrating a great joy.

On my forty-first birthday this year, I received a heavy package in the mail from Lynn Morrissey. I opened it up and could not believe it. Each AttaGirl, and a couple of AttaGuy friends as well, had written a tribute or a memory and a birthday wish to me! It's the most precious gift I've ever received, and I keep it to re-read when I'm having a low-self-esteem day. In addition, I received a beautiful oil painting print. In the center of the painting is an old-fashioned inkwell, a feather pen, and a white piece of paper. Upon closer inspection, I realized that there were words on that paper—words of love and gratitude signed, believe it or not, "The AttaGirls." If anything, these AttaChicks are creative and amazingly generous with their love and affection.

This spring, before the convention, we met at Cracker Barrel for breakfast and talked of how hard it was for each of us to enter the Christian publishing industry at first, and of the grain-of-sand-on-the-publishing-beach feeling we all encountered, especially at the annual convention. Until this particular year, the ever-gregarious and generous Liz Curtis Higgs had invited established authors and speakers such as Kay Arthur, Patsy Clairmont, Carol Kent, Lee Ezell, and many others to an annual brunch as a gift of encouragement to us in the field. It had turned into a real highlight for those who attended, making us feel less alone and more fully supported in our individual ministries. Sadly, our beloved Lizzy's schedule was such that she could not hostess the brunch this year, and we just couldn't imagine the convention without the Liz & Friends event. We also knew of several other new authors who would be coming this year—without a friend and without support—and so we pitched in during Liz's absence (with her gracious blessing) and together we hosted an AttaGirl Brunch.

This year's purpose was for established authors to welcome "newbies" into our fold. All the AttaGirls pitched in, I hosting it with my newly broken arm. (And heavily drugged with pain medication. I'm still wondering what I said.)

Carol Kent, who is a beloved friend and speaking teacher to all the AttaGirls, and president of Speak Up Speaker Services, shared ten quick ways to be more effective when speaking in front of a group. In true Carol form, she kept the 40 or so of us in the hotel meeting room spellbound. (Carol is another friend who deserves a whole chapter of her own. She's given so unselfishly of her time and knowledge to me and my AttaFriends. She's had one of those years that deserves at least a T-shirt to celebrate surviving, and yet, in the midst of her own pain, she continues to rise up and give and give and give to whomever God brings her way. I've never met anyone who knows Carol Kent who doesn't comment, "Is she not the most gracious, kind woman you've ever met?" She's Jesus with skin on to hundreds of women who love her dearly.)

Then our own Velveteen Woman, Brenda, closed the morning with tender, quiet, and poignant thoughts like, "How much is enough? Are you taking time for yourselves to let God love you, so you can pour out that love? Do you need to pull away more often and snuggle up with Him to keep yourself from burning out?"

It was a wonderful, warm success that has snowballed into other authors getting inspired to join in the mentoring process. Next year, there's a whole weekend of festivities and workshops planned for new authors and speakers. (I get to host the PJ party!)

Sometimes I feel like a grandmother must feel at a family reunion as she sits back in her rocker and observes her kids and her kids' kids interacting and playing horseshoes, or laughing together as they lick frosting from a bowl. I see all these dear, talented women writers as my literary children of sorts (even though some are older than I!) and watch in pure delight as they began to soar on their own, form friendships among themselves, and—better yet—start to mentor new wannabe writers. It's a miracle and one of the most satisfying, ongoing joys of my life.

And to think it all started with one small girlfriend chat over French coffee and Caesar salads at La Madeline's—and one ding-a-ling suitcase full of colored pictures and heartfelt words, bound together with a few naïve hopes and prayers and dreams.

From the days when God picked a little shepherd boy to slay a giant, and the smallest, weakest tribe of Israel to produce the King of kings—it always amazes me how the Lord seems to especially enjoy using the foolish to confound the wise and selecting the Least Likely to Succeed to accomplish His will on this planet.

When He puts a small cluster of women together and gives them a purpose greater than themselves—watch out. The world is about to change, one AttaWoman at a time.

Has God given you a seed of a dream, my friend? One that both excites and scares you just a little bit? Dare to walk outside the safe house of your comfort zone to the fertile soil of your future. Once there, plant your thought seeds, and tend and water your dreams. And as you work and walk in The Garden Where Dreams Come True, don't forget to take a bunch of good girlfriends along with you.

You'll especially appreciate their help and cheering come harvest time.

In the morning sow your seed,
and in the evening do not withhold your hand;
for you do not know which will prosper, either this or that,
or whether both alike will be good.
ECCLESIASTES 11:6 NKJV

"Become so wrapped up in something
that you forget to be afraid."
—Lady Bird Johnson, *Women Say the Wisest Things*

AttaGirl Web sites!

If you'd like to take a peek at what we're up to, here's my list of AttaGirl authors' Web sites!

Becky: **www.beckyfreeman.com** (check my great reads & links page where I have all of the AttaGirls books pictured and listed)

Ellie: **www.elliekay.com**

Jane: **www.janejarrell.com**

Kali: **www.trufflesfromheaven.com**

Gracie: **www.graciemalone.com**

AttaGirl All-Pitch-In Salad

(A Freeman family favorite! I used to beg my mother to make this on Friday nights with hotdogs or hamburgers.)

For a Luncheon: You can assign girlfriends to bring one ingredient each and then put this salad together as you visit. Serve with a loaf of bread and sliced cantaloupe as an easy, yummy luncheon. (Why not host a Creativity Support Group Salad Luncheon where you can begin to encourage each other to tend and grow your dreams?)

1 head lettuce, torn in bite-size pieces
1 tomato, chopped
1 can Ranch Style beans, rinsed and drained
2 c. grated cheese
½ c. chopped green onions
1 small bag of Fritos corn chips
1 bottle Catalina Dressing (or Catalina Light)
(May add 1 lb. seasoned, cooked, drained, and cooled ground beef to make this a meal.)

Toss first five ingredients in a large salad bowl. Keep chilled. Just before serving add corn chips and dressing.

8

"We Have to Help..."

Good Samaritan Friends

The phone rang one afternoon in May. I answered it and grinned when I heard the thick Texas drawl of my old friend Brenda Scott. (Not to be confused with Brenda Waggoner, Velveteen Woman. It's odd that two of my best friends are both named Brenda!)

"Hi, Becky," she said, only it came out in three syllables— "Bayuhky."

"Hey, Brenda!" I exclaimed. "Great to hear from you. What are you up to?"

"Way-uhl," she began, "I'm trying to save somebody's life."

I blinked involuntarily, then shook my head and laughed. "Oh, is that all?" Nothing Brenda would say or do could surprise me very much. After all, we had history together.

Brenda and I had shared laughs and tears over more than 20 years. As teenage newlywed wives (going to college classes alongside our newlywed husbands), we'd butchered many a recipe together, desperate to be the Betty Crockers our mothers had been. Combining our efforts one day in the late 1970s, we whipped up a batch of chocolate cookies and served them with eager anticipation to our young, hungry hubbies. They each took a big bite, began to chew, then ran in tandem toward the kitchen sink and a glass of water—spitting and hollering as they went.

Brenda had accidentally substituted salt for the sugar!

We still laugh at the memory of the night Brenda made and served her grandmother's Buttermilk Pie to our young couples Bible study group. "Wait 'till y'all taste it," she'd happily assured us. "It's my favorite pie and it doesn't taste anything like buttermilk." And it probably would not have, had she cooked it all the way through. As it was, runny and oh-so-sour-milky in the middle, she had another gagging, spitting stampede to the kitchen sink on her hands.

Brenda and I had cleaned each other's houses, played 42 (a dominos game) with our spouses until midnight (on a newlywed's budget, we went for cheap entertainment), and prayed each other through marital adjustments, semester tests, and babies' births. It surprised everyone who knew Brenda and me, the most scatterbrained women friends on God's planet, to discover that we were both rather amazingly book smart. I, of course, have used all my book smarts to write literal books about my scatterbrained life. Despite Brenda's easy ability to laugh at her own foibles (of which there are many)—and the fact that she'll never write a Betty Crocker Cookbook Sequel—Brenda holds the lives of other people in her hands everyday. She's a skilled and compassionate nurse in a large modern hospital, and so when she said, "I'm trying to save somebody's life"—I assumed she was talking about one of her patients.

But I was soon to discover this case was altogether unique.

"Becky, I'm stepping out on faith like I've never done before," Brenda said. "And I may be wasting my time and spinning my wheels but I feel, more strongly than I've ever felt about anything, that I need to do everything I can to save my new friend's life."

I sat down on the edge of my bed. "Who is she?" I asked. "What's wrong?"

Brenda sighed before starting into her story. "Remember when I felt God's assurance that I was to go to Bulgaria on a short-term mission trip, even though I was scared to death?"

"Yes," I replied. "And I remember how afraid you were—with other people supporting you financially and with their prayers—that you'd go and come back from Bulgaria without making an impact. You kept saying that over and over. 'What if I don't make an impact?' Of course, all of us who know and love you knew what a ridiculous question that was. You don't go anywhere, around anybody, without making an impact."

"I know, Becky," Brenda laughed as she spoke. "But what KIND of impact would I make? I wanted so badly to touch lives while I was there, to put away my own selfish thoughts, and to be used by God."

"And?"

"You just won't believe it," Brenda answered, her voice nearly breaking with emotion. "To our surprise, the Bulgarians asked us to preach at their church services. Now I never talk in front of groups, but we just said what was on our hearts and performed nine services in eleven days. At the end of our time there, one of the Bulgarian pastors told us that we had affected his people in a remarkable way, encouraging them and loving them in Christ as never before."

"Oh, my," I said gently. "What did you all say to all that?"

"Becky, I literally couldn't say anything. I just felt my head getting heavier as I laid it down on the table in front of me and wept for joy. God has used me. ME!"

I smiled, a lump forming in my own throat as I said to my dear friend, "Brenda, I think you've always underestimated yourself—but God has never underestimated you."

"Well, I think I may be in way over my head this time."

"What's going on?"

Brenda's voice grew quieter, serious. "While we were in Bulgaria, I met this incredible woman named Bonka."

"Bonka?"

"Yes, don't you love that name? Anyway, she's been on kidney dialysis for ten years and she just can't stay on it for too much longer. She desperately needs a transplant to live. Her pastor tells us that she's such a beacon of joy in that church. Her husband and teenage daughter adore her. But Bulgaria is not like America. Over there: no money, no charity. She will simply die without the money for a kidney transplant. For some reason beyond myself, I just feel like I'm supposed to get involved in helping to raise funds and get Bonka a transplant. But I have no earthly idea where to begin."

"How can I help?" I asked.

"Well, I read in your *Real Magnolias* book about your friend Melissa giving her kidney to a neighbor's child and I'd just like to talk to her about the whole procedure and possibly get some medical contacts and networking going. And I want to brainstorm with you about how to raise funds."

"Hey," I said, "I'm no Barbara Johnson—but I do have a pretty good number of fans and friends in the Dallas area.

How about we use my name and offer a night of laughter and encouragement at a large Dallas church—with the proceeds from an offering going to Bonka. How much do you need to raise?"

"It looks like we need about $20,000 altogether."

"Okay, I'll call the folks at KCBI radio. They've been so good to me about doing interviews for my books. Let's see if they'll let me do a short interview and advertise the event."

Brenda sounded encouraged. "Yes, and then I'll send out letters to area pastors."

"Great!" I said, then paused before adding, "Brenda, I'm so proud of you."

"But what if all my efforts fail? What if this is a waste of time? What if I get Bonka's hopes up only to have them dashed—and what if she dies?"

"Then she will have died knowing she had one American girlfriend who loved her and cared enough to try to help. You have nothing in terms of worldly esteem or profit to gain from this, and it's going to cost you tons of time and red tape, plus leaping the hurdle of a language barrier. But if God has put this in your heart, what choice do you have but to follow through and leave the results to Him?"

And so, a few short weeks later, Brenda and I showed up at a large metropolitan church ready for the event of a lifetime: Becky and Brenda Going Bonkers for Bonka. With my popular name on the marquee of this fundraiser, who knew how many people might show up? Hundreds? Thousands?

How about fewer than thirty.

Every speaker should have the opportunity, at least once in their lifetime, to look out over a huge auditorium of seats, with a handful of people scattered here and there trying their best to look like a throng. I once read that Grady Wilson said of his friend Billy Graham, "If God will keep Billy anointed, we'll keep him humble." God seems to be really great at keeping me humble, with or without the help of my friends. Now all I could do was pray that God would not spare His anointing on the tiny audience in the great big church.

He didn't. For from that unlikely, miniscule audience, God raised over $4,000 for Bonka's transplant. A solid start.

Periodically—over a long and grueling, heartlifting and heartbreaking 18-month period—I'd get updates from Brenda on the progress made. Or not made. Interspersed with those were charming notes from Bonka herself and Stephan, her husband—written in their own dear way of speaking English. They always signed their notes to Brenda, "God bless and bag you reachly." We think it meant, "God bless you and bring you richly" but we're not sure. It was just such an adorable sign-off that Brenda never mentioned the misspelling and mispronunciation, the same way we don't correct our kids when they pronounce spaghetti "buhs-ketti." Why change something that makes you smile?

Excerpts from their e-mails and Brenda's appeals read like a poignant journal.

> *Dear Brenda,*
>
> *Ever days in mai life is danger situation, but I feel the love of my brothers and sisters and how beautiful is the blessing. Aur Lord giving my peace in the heart. Please pray for me I need to have God's patience! Some time I fill the difficult time to the wait for. I know God will came just in time, He neva late! God Bless and Bag You Reachly, Stephan and Boni.*

> Dear Friends,
>
> Suppose a brother or sister is without clothes and daily food (or a functioning kidney). "If one of you says to

him, 'Go, I wish you well; keep warm and well fed,' but does nothing about his physical needs, what good is it?" I am simply a housewife who has never done fundraising before. We have raised $12,000 so far—evidence that this is God's work, because we are really out of our area of expertise!

I beg you to consider this need of a sister in Christ. She is only one person, but God esteemed her highly enough to send us 5,000 miles to meet her and discover her need.

Thank you, Brenda Scott.

I know How is my Savior I'm not fright of death. I believe in the promises of aur God and He know how difficult is the condition here to waite and using dialysis like my in Bulgaria. I'm really happy that I have you brothers and sisters arount me to take cary of me in your prayers. God bless you and bag you reachly! Stephan and Bonka.

Dear Friends of Bonka,

One woman, a missionary/nurse, told us that to have Bonka's operation done in Russia, with their lack of high-quality equipment and care, is to give her a death sentence. Pray for a way to get Bonka to America. A local hospital has agreed to perform the surgery if we can get her here. She can stay with me until a kidney becomes available. Thanks, Brenda Scott.

Over the phone, Brenda described the agonies, paperwork, and hours of phone calls simply to get Bonka's blood to the U.S. to be tested. Nothing came easy, every step was difficult, and the perseverance required to be Bonka's advocate was nothing short of supernatural. She'd often describe the process as "peeling an onion" little by little, uncovering one thin skin of hope at a time.

Soon Bonka was waiting, ticket in hand, to come to America for the transplant when, at the last minute, legal red tape and medical difficulties prevented her coming. It was a heartbreaking moment when all seemed lost, and Bonka—with tear-stained face—had to wave good-bye at the airport to the people who had come to take her to America, her last hope of living to see her daughter grow up seemingly dashed.

When I'd question Brenda, "How are you hanging in there with so many disappointments?" she'd always give me two answers. "I cannot write Bonka and say, 'I give up.' I simply cannot do that to her or her family. And God always gives us just enough encouragement to keep us keeping on."

Indeed He did, as another e-mail from Brenda to friends demonstrated.

Dear Friends,

I was allowed to make a request for money for Bonka's transplant at my church this morning. At this point, we have seen every door closed for Bonka to come to America and have received some reassurance that she will get good care in St. Petersburg, Russia. But with the devaluing of the ruble, we still need more money—about $25,000. There were about 100 women in the Bible study this morning. They told me I could only speak for three minutes to let them know about Bonka and her need. Would you believe that after only three minutes, those women gave $6,065 for Bonka?!?

—Brenda

(One man wrote Brenda back and said, "At $2,000 a minute, we need to have you speaking a lot!" Brenda quickly responded that this was a 100 percent pure, one-time, God Thing and she wasn't planning to turn fundraising into a career.)

Then came the glorious day when Brenda's faith became sight, the clouds of doubt rolled back like a scroll. And all who had witnessed her perseverance stood in amazement at what God had done through one woman on behalf of another woman friend.

"Dear Brenda," came the e-mailed news from Stephan. *"Bonka already has been transplant. The surgery have been successful..."* (Can you hear the cymbals crash? Can you hear the angels sing?)

And then, after the kidney began working on its own and Bonka was out of the rejection woods, came this note from the grateful recipient of the gift of life that Brenda and hundreds of unknown friends an ocean away had given.

> *Brenda, I am doing so well! We all want to see you and aur prayers is to see you again face to face. We love you so much! We believe that God will bag you and your family more blessing in your life. All is possible in the name of Jesus.*

A few months later, a plane from America landed in the small, poverty-tinged country of Bulgaria. Out from the plane walked my friend Brenda—just an ordinary woman—into the waiting arms of Stephan and a new, improved, dialysis-free Bonka. They needed no language to express their gratitude and mutual joy at what God had wrought between them.

Stephan and Bonka and the church in Bulgaria treated Brenda like a queen or an angel, something so foreign to

Brenda's way of looking at herself that it seemed comical to her.

But who's to say that true girlfriends, who carry your burdens in their heart, and show their love through action, are not queens and angels both? They may look like regular blend-into-the-crowd housewives who spend most of their time chaperoning kids or washing clothes. They do not wear crowns or sport wings of shimmering white and gold. In fact, their uniform of choice is usually blue jeans and tennis shoes. (Or in Brenda's case, a nurse's uniform.)

However, in spite of their average appearance, you can still tell a true angel/queen friend by one distinguishing item of dress.

They wear their heart—as big as a Father's love—on their sleeve.

She opens her arms to the poor and extends her hands to the needy.... She is clothed with strength and dignity.
PROVERBS 31:20,25

"*We can do no great things, only small things with great love.*"
—Mother Teresa, *Women Say the Wisest Things*

Friends to the Finish Line

A few years ago, at the Seattle Special Olympics, nine contestants, all physically or mentally disabled, assembled at the starting line for the 100-yard dash.

At the gun, they all started out, not exactly in a dash, but with a relish to run the race to the finish and win. All, that is, except one little boy who stumbled on the asphalt, tumbled over a couple of times, and began to cry.

The other eight heard the boy cry. They slowed down and looked back.

Then they all turned around and went back.

Every one of them.

One girl with Down syndrome bent down and kissed him and said: "This will make it better."

Then all nine linked arms and walked together to the finish line.

Everyone in the stadium stood, and the cheering went on for several minutes. People who were there are still telling the story.

Because deep down we know this one thing: What matters in this life is more than winning for ourselves. What matters in this life is helping others win, even if it means slowing down and changing our course.

Becky's Best Banana Bread

(Perfect for Sharing with a Hurting Friend)

8 T. butter (I use Smart Balance, one of those butters made with good-for-your-heart oils)

¾ c. Sucanat (a natural sugar) or brown sugar

2 eggs

1 c. unbleached flour

1 t. baking soda

1 c. whole wheat flour

3 large ripe bananas (or 4 small ones) mashed

1 t. vanilla

½ c. chopped pecans or walnuts

Heat oven to 350 degrees.

Cream butter, sugar, and eggs. Sift flours with baking soda. (Wheat germ will sift out of whole wheat flour, but just toss it back in the bowl! That's the best part!) Add nuts.

Stir into creamed mixture. Fold in bananas and vanilla. You can bake this in a loaf pan for about 50 minutes or until a cake tester comes out clean.

I like to bake this in a small oblong pan. (It cooks much faster—20 to 30 minutes, and makes for even, smaller, easier-to-handle slices.) Then I can cut it in half, keep one for my family, then give the other half—wrapped in foil and laid on a pretty paper plate—to a neighbor in need.

How Old Am I??

April 16, 1999 was my birthday. This much I know. However, what I did not know that year was how old I was going to be. This e-mail came from my detailed sister as she was trying to determine my real age for the AttaGirls wanting to give me a birthday gift.

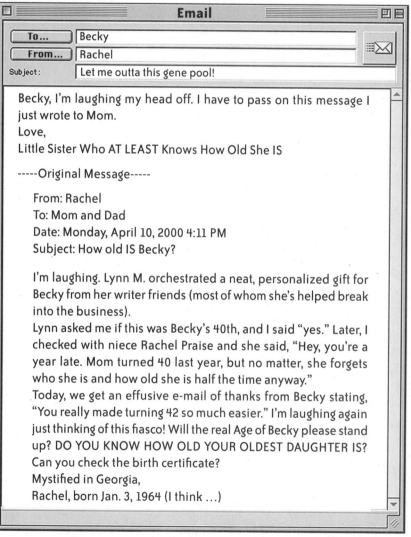

Email

To... | Becky
From... | Rachel
Subject: | Let me outta this gene pool!

Becky, I'm laughing my head off. I have to pass on this message I just wrote to Mom.
Love,
Little Sister Who AT LEAST Knows How Old She IS

-----Original Message-----

From: Rachel
To: Mom and Dad
Date: Monday, April 10, 2000 4:11 PM
Subject: How old IS Becky?

I'm laughing. Lynn M. orchestrated a neat, personalized gift for Becky from her writer friends (most of whom she's helped break into the business).
Lynn asked me if this was Becky's 40th, and I said "yes." Later, I checked with niece Rachel Praise and she said, "Hey, you're a year late. Mom turned 40 last year, but no matter, she forgets who she is and how old she is half the time anyway."
Today, we get an effusive e-mail of thanks from Becky stating, "You really made turning 42 so much easier." I'm laughing again just thinking of this fiasco! Will the real Age of Becky please stand up? DO YOU KNOW HOW OLD YOUR OLDEST DAUGHTER IS? Can you check the birth certificate?
Mystified in Georgia,
Rachel, born Jan. 3, 1964 (I think ...)

Author's Note: Mystery Solved: I was born in 1959. I've recalculated that figure and have determined I am actually 29 years old. And holding. ☺

Part IV

▲ ▼ ▲

Let's Hear It for the Boys!

When Guy Friends
Rate up There with Girlfriends

9

"How Can I Help YOU Succeed?"

Mentoring Friends

I opened the package from a publisher without much thought. After seven plus years of writing and making friends in this business, I get lots of books in the mail. But when I pulled this hardback volume out of the envelope and saw the title, and my friend's name underneath it written in rich gold and black, I slowly drew in a long breath, sat down, and cried.

The title of the book is *Final Roar*, a follow-up to the groundbreaking *Roaring Lambs*. The Texas-born author, Bob Briner, spent the last of his 64 earth years "walking in tall cotton," as we say in our home state—rubbing elbows with most of today's top sports giants, negotiating with many of the world's wealthiest businessmen, befriending well-known musicians and artists, and roaring the gospel with the gentleness of a lamb.

But I didn't cry because the world has lost a great influential man, Robert A. Briner. I cried because I miss my friend,

Bob, a lamb who went to be with his Shepherd one early summer's day in 1999. This final book was compiled from notes and chapters written during Bob's final brave days battling cancer. He finally conceded a loss to the disease but claimed victory in Jesus to his last breath.

I read his encouraging e-mails, his kind notes, his advice-filled faxes, and got the feeling that somebody big and smart and tough and gentle was looking out for me, like a brother or an uncle—a Roaring Lamb King.

I read the first pages of *Final Roar*, filled with tributes from others. But, of course, I scanned past the others' comments to read my own words first. (I think our eyes are automatically drawn to what we've produced, as surely as a child is drawn to observe the bean she planted in her own paper cup. Though there may be many other well-deserving bean plants sprouting beside ours on life's windowsill, we stay most intrigued with our own cups, no matter how grown up we get.)

Through my tears, I read what I'd written a few months before.

"Bob Briner, CEO, Emmy Award Winner, and friend of many rich and famous, treated me, an unknown new writer, the way he treated everyone, as if they were God's special child. Ever charming and self-deprecating, he'd often sign his notes to me, 'From Your Chubby Pal.' I met Bob through his first book, *Roaring Lambs*, which I considered a turning point treatise in my life. I wrote him a fan letter and he called back. From the beginning he took a mentoring, fatherly role, advising, befriending, praying for my family and me. Though he is absent in the body, I hear the echo of Bob's guiding words in almost every decision I make for my ministry and career. 'Keep a close circle of friends who aren't overly impressed with you, who'll be honest and who'll pray for you.' 'Write to everyone who writes you, return calls as soon as humanly possible.' 'Make sure your business dealings are Christ-like, and don't be deceived by those calling them-selves Christians who are being unethical in their dealings.' 'Be salt, be light, be you.' I miss The Big Guy."

Satisfied with what had been printed, I turned the pages to see other familiar names and read their tributes. Many Christian musicians, straining to light a world outside the subculture of the church, were on the list of Bob's men-torees. Margaret Becker wrote, "He was anointed. He was real. He was free. And I was changed as a result." Stephen Curtis Chapman summed up our mutual friend's generosity of spirit by saying, "Bob Briner was so selfless in his giving. If I asked him for his input on something, he would inun-date me with information and at the end of each message he would say, 'No need to respond to this—just know that I'm praying for you and know that I love you.' He so well mir-rored what I think Jesus' friendship should be like." Michael W. Smith paid him perhaps the highest compliment a man could give another man. "Other than my own father and pastor, I have never had another man encourage me the way Bob did. He was 100 percent servant, and I am a better, wiser man because of his impact on my life."

I recognized name after name: Cal Thomas, the nationally syndicated columnist; Johnny Hart, cartoonist and creator of *B.C.* and *Wizard of Id*; Ken Wales, producer of the television show *Christy*; and Dave Dravecky, former pitcher for the San Francisco Giants; the alternative rock group Jars of Clay, along with several CEOs, college presidents, writers, artists, and musicians.

I had two thoughts after scanning the list of Bob Briner's buddies. The first thought was similar to a question Bob asked himself in his introduction to *Roaring Lambs*. Referring to meeting the Shah of Iran, chatting with Mike Wallace on Air-Iran, riding in a Tokyo limo with the founder of Sony, being part of the front office at Shea Stadium, and negotiating with sharp businessmen atop Caesars Palace, Bob had asked himself, "What am I, a product of a modest public school system and two small Christian colleges *doing* here?" When I look over the list of CEOs, lawyers, producers, actors, writers, and artists that penned their praises to Bob's memory, I ask myself, "What am I, a humor writer and mom from the woods of East Texas *doing* in this list?"

The second thought I had was similar to what we kids felt when we discovered that mom and dad loved our brothers and sisters as much as they loved us. I wonder if each of us, in some part of our childlike psyches, thought we were The Special Friend of Bob's—only to discover his love knew no bounds. As the sports editor of the *Miami Herald* so aptly described Bob: "There is no greater praise than this: Everyone who knew him well considered him their best friend."

Though I've read every book Bob has written, and visited with him in person and by phone many times, I still scratch my head and ask, "How did he DO that? How did he make so many feel they were his best friend?"

How, indeed, did one incredibly busy man with a major business to run, a loving family, and a full writing, media, and speaking schedule manage to pull it off? How did this modern King Arthur inspire a Round Table of loyal friends to be bright and shining beacons—to bring a bit of Christian Camelot to a dark, hurting world?

It's a question I wanted answers to, if I was to become the sort of friend Jesus wants me to be.

I once asked my friend Coyle Stephenson, "Coyle, in all your years of ministry—being a pastor, a chaplain of children's home and hospitals, and counseling other pastors—what have you learned about people?"

To this question, Coyle, made wise by years and experience, answered simply, "The truth? We're all just so hungry for a little affirmation."

This is what Bob gave so generously—the gift of affirmation. His "attaboy"s and "attagirl"s given with consistency and creativity—through word and deed—fed the souls of many discouraged and starving artists. He entered a room with an attitude that said, "There *you* are!" and not "Here *I* am!"

His example of affirming by responding—quickly, enthusiastically—is one of the main reasons I answer every phone call, every e-mail, and every letter. It's why I write dozens of notes and thank you's, saving time in my schedule for this (Mondays are correspondence days). Being naturally scatterbrained, I sometimes lose or overlook a piece of correspondence—but I do try, and I'll keep trying. I'll say "no" to some income-producing opportunities to keep my schedule free to be as responsive and available as I humanly can, especially to my family and my dozen closest friends. Bob's mentoring is one of the reasons that when someone asks me, "What is your goal in life?" I answer with this one answer: "To treat everyone God puts in my path as if they are precious—which they are."

Another "How to Be a Great Friend" observation worth noting: Bob Briner gave affirmation from a position of a humble servant, not as some Great Spiritual One who agreed to acknowledge the Lowly Underlings with a compliment. Though he had every reason to command the utmost respect, to be called "Mister" and "Sir," he signed his notes with hilarious, self-effacing signatures. A very large man (before cancer reduced him to slimness the hard way), Bob ended his notes to his protégés with signature humor. To me, he signed off as "Your Chubby Pal." To Barry Landis (VP of Atlantic Records and one of two friends who helped finish *Final Roar*), Bob was the "Tubby Texan." Bill Herring, President Emeritus of Knickerbocker Artists, wrote from his heart, "I'm still broken up. I had lost hope that such men existed. Some men shoot off a rocket of truth just by the way they sign their names. Bob used to sign his letters to me with 'El Blobo.' Every time he did that, it changed my life. So good to think my life could be changed."

I suspect one of the things Bob liked and saw in me was that I'd made a whole ministry and career out of making messes and writing about them. (His lovely wife, Marty, was a true fan of *Worms in My Tea*.) Perhaps it was in this tendency to openly admit my own flaws and laugh about them (a form of humor Bob also employed) that he saw I had potential to reach people for Christ whom others might intimidate. (One thing I've never been accused of is making *anyone* feel intimidated.) So if Bob was the Chubby Pal, I was the Ditzy Gal.

There's always a thought, a philosophy, behind why we behave the way we do. Behind every action is a reason. Why did Bob treat young artists so kindly? Why did he generously pass on professional lessons gleaned, that others might have hoarded? Why didn't he view the young and upcoming "stars" as threats to his ego?

It began with his *Roaring Lambs* philosophy. Bob's basic premise of how to best, most strategically, affect the world for Christ was to light a candle rather than to shout at the darkness. Bob was a practical man and he embraced this philosophy for practical reasons: He believed this was Christ's method, and it worked better. We attract more bees with honey than vinegar. We introduce people to the love of

Christ by being salty and flavorful as we sprinkle our way through the Real World—refusing to hide behind the safe gates of our Christian communities.

Taking this public stand was not without its price, and Bob wasn't always admired or embraced for what he'd come to so firmly believe. For example, he openly criticized Christians and organizations who, in his words, "wasted their time" protesting the world's entertainment industry for doing what a world without Christian influence will naturally do, especially when we abandon the Hollywood Ship to live on a Christians-Only Island. He proposed that we quickly regroup our "I'm Against (fill in the blank)" mentality and redirect our thoughts toward positive efforts: supporting students, artists, and business men and women who are willing to hone their craft, and with our friendship and prayers, encourage them to enter the worlds of Disney, Hollywood, Washington, and Wall Street with top-notch skills, uncompromising integrity, and a lifestyle that honors and speaks of Christ. To shepherd lambs that will roar; to make long-lasting changes in our world from the inside out, rather than by becoming some caricature of The Angry Christian, so preoccupied with being "outraged" that we cannot find time for sharing good news and compassion with the objects of our fury.

Not only did Bob respond, personally and quickly, to others, but he also poured out his affection in abundance, going way beyond the call of duty. Barry Landis told about faxing Bob a note about how much he enjoyed *Roaring Lambs*. To Barry's shock, Bob faxed him back within the same day. When Barry said he was coming to Dallas, Bob offered to pick him up at the airport and take him to one of the nicest restaurants in town. (If anything, Bob was always First Class.)

Now, I can understand Bob's generous response to Barry—after all, Barry is in a terrific position of influence with a major record label.

But consider this: In 1993, I was a new author; my book had not even debuted. I wrote Bob a fan letter after reading *Roaring Lambs*. Within five days, the phone rang. "Becky," the friendly voice said, "Hey, this is Bob Briner and I called to thank you for that wonderful letter." He engaged me in couldn't-be-friendlier chitchat, while I was sweating bullets on the other end of the line thinking, *This is an EMMY AWARD-WINNING PRODUCER!* Then he said, "You know, Marty and I would love to take you and Scott out to dinner next Thursday. Would you mind driving to Dallas next week?"

Mind? Well, of course, I had to check my busy schedule (washing clothes, making beds, wiping noses) but quickly assessed that Scott and I could probably squeeze Mr. and Mrs. Briner into our schedules.

Thursday evening, after meeting the Briners and getting a quick tour of their home (which included a stop at a portrait of their beautiful kids and grandkids, as well as a glance at that Emmy), Bob drove us to Café Pacific in Highland Park. He treated us to an amazing meal that included—of course!—a fabulous chocolate-layered torte. The meal cost more than we could have spent on a week's worth of groceries for our family of six—it was the sort of dinner we loved but could never have afforded in those days of raising little ones on one paycheck.

One day, months later, the phone rang. It was Bob's secretary calling to ask our address—Bob had caught a salmon in Alaska and wanted to ship it to us overnight for our family to enjoy. Hanging up the phone, all I could think of was that this incredibly important man had caught a fish and—

for who knows what reason—thought of our family and wanted to share his catch with us. Jesus did that once, you know—caught some fish, cooked them up, and shared them with his friends. Bob often seemed to be doing things Jesus would do, and sometimes he did it by just showing up.

At the Christian Bookseller's Association Convention one year, I had what I call my Annual CBA Cry: it comes from exhaustion and feeling amazingly insignificant after seeing your precious little books are just grains of sand on the bookselling beach. I walked outside and around a corner, to the back of a building, where I could let go with a good sob in solitude. Seemingly out of nowhere walked Bob right into my Pity Party. He wasn't a big hugger but he patted my back and said all the things you'd want a big brother to say. "Who hurt your feelings? Anybody I need to talk to? These people can be so unfeeling sometimes...."

"No, no, no," I said between sobs, "I'm just having a CBA breakdown and I'm tired and I'm a woman."

He just nodded, gave me his card, and said, "Now, you call me if you need anything."

Christmas of 1998, I was thinking about Bob—hadn't heard from the big guy in a few months, which was unusual. But he'd moved from Dallas to Greenville, Illinois, so the move and the distance and our ever-busier lives lessened our correspondence some. So I e-mailed him, thanking him for his latest book and his personal encouragement.

He responded with a short, "Becky, so good to hear from you. Can't write much. Very weak. But through a chemo fog, I'm still seeing Jesus."

I hadn't heard. I called Marty, and she told me of a football-sized tumor found and removed from Bob's abdomen. She was optimistic then, and so was I.

But by the spring of 1999, things were not going well—at least in the physical realm. I called and asked Bob if I could visit him in May. "We'd love to see you," he said. And so on a beautiful day in late spring, with my husband's encouragement, I drove up from Paducah, where I had been speaking, to see the Briners in Illinois. On the morning of the planned visit, I'd called to make sure he was feeling up to seeing me. I remember so well his exact words. "Becky, I *urge* you to come." What he didn't say, but what we both knew he meant, was, "This may be our last face-to-face visit before I go Home."

"I'm on my way, Bob," I answered.

Marty, Bob's beautiful wife, and Leigh, one of Bob's lovely daughters, answered the door. I brought a basket of books and tapes and gave them to Marty—who loves to laugh, even through tears. Bob came in dressed from head to toe in black: black sweats, black turtleneck, and a black baseball cap to cover his head now bald from chemotherapy. He was thin by now, and he was especially pale from the treatments and from staying indoors. I might not have recognized him at all if it weren't for his familiar, gentle voice. Marty, ever strong and quiet, wiped away unbidden tears as she talked of Bob's courage, kindness, uncomplaining ways, and of the news they'd just received that the last round of treatments had not stopped the insidious cancer. She loved this man so very much and oh, how he loved her. Marty, perhaps, has been the bravest roaring lamb of all.

We chatted, and though I tried to steer the conversation to Bob and how he was doing and what projects he was working on, true to form he continued to ask about me. There he was, weak and dying—but he smiled and gave all he had: his kind and rapt attention.

When I stood to leave I wanted to hug Bob, but I'd had a cold and I didn't want to chance weakening his delicate immune system. So I walked over to him as close as I dared and said, "I'll see you again, my friend. I love you, and Scott and I are praying for you." He smiled weakly up at me—serene as a still lake on a quiet evening—and said the last words I ever heard him say, "Thank you for coming, Becky. We'll see each other again and whether it is here or in heaven, I want you to know it is really okay with me." I swallowed a lump threatening to form in my throat.

Then Leigh hopped in my rental car and took me for a tour of Bob's beloved alma mater—Greenville College—and the room that had been dedicated to her father's work on behalf of the Christian university. Afterwards, I dropped her off and as I drove around their house, I saw Bob—outside! It was the most peaceful picture. The sun was shining down on his upturned face as he sat basking in its warmth. I slowed the car down, rolled down the window, and waved. He lifted one long arm up slowly, smiled under the shade of his ball cap, and waved a final good-bye.

Within a few short weeks, our gentle giant, our Roaring Lamb, went home.

But those of us that remain behind have not forgotten, will never forget, the incredible honor it was to be called a friend of Bob's.

Can you hear us roar?

They will follow the Lord; he will roar like a lion.
When he roars, his children will come....
HOSEA 11:10

"*Quietly and stealthily he walked among us, making tracks in the culture and then in our little pen of subculture. When fully surrounded by woolly silence, he let out a magnificent roar, full of love and anguish, hope and frustration. The power of his roar startled me out through the gate, and the truth of his roar has kept me out. Second only to the Lion of Judah, Lamb of God, this roaring servant leader has changed my world.*"

—Nicole Johnson, actress and author

Friendship as Sacrament?

In Terry Hershey's book on intimacy, *Go Away, Come Closer: When What You Need the Most Is What You Fear the Most,* there's a wonderful chapter entitled "Friendship, Community, and Liturgy." Here I pass onto you, my friends, some of my favorite thoughts gleaned from that chapter. For, though most of my writing about friendship in this book is fun and lighthearted, I want to emphasize one thing in all seriousness:

- God created us to need each other.

- Without one or two friends, we will simply dry up and die in this world. None of us were created to be Lone Rangers.

- NOTHING, other than your relationship with God, is as important as planting and tending family relationships and friendships.

"The bottom line is unavoidable. We cannot handle life on our own. We need friends. Granted, self-sufficiency is our preference. But we need friends. We may not have a good track record in this area. But we need friends. Friends—real friends—may be difficult to find. But we need friends. Because life was not meant to be handled on our own."

About Dan Jansen, the American speed skater who met disaster by falling in both Olympic advents he had entered, Hershey writes:

"In an image difficult to forget, the television cameras froze on Dan as he was being consoled by his girlfriend after the second fall....I was drawn to the comment of a sportswriter from Los Angeles who wrote, 'Dan Jansen did not have a medal around his neck, but he did have her. He had someone who wanted to hold him tight, someone to say everything is OK....' "[7]

Keep on investing in your relationships, make time in your calendar for them—for there will come a day when you'll fall and can't get up without the helping hands of those who love you.

Bread Multiplied and Glorified

A Southern-style Bread Pudding
with Hard Sauce
(From Jim and Shirley, our favorite B&B owners
of The Rose Garden Bed & Breakfast, Nashville,
Tennessee. This is a melt-in-your mouth specialty
of Jim's. I love the way bread pudding takes on a
second life as older bread is broken and used
again. It says something to me about how giving
away the pieces of our broken lives, results in a
brand new creation. A regeneration of life!)

1 loaf stale French bread

5 eggs, well beaten

1 c. sugar

2 T. vanilla

1 c. pecan pieces

1 c. raisins

1 ½ - 2 cups milk (depends on staleness of the bread)
cinnamon and nutmeg

½ stick butter

Break bread into chunks. Add rest of ingredients—adding the milk last, adding more milk
until bread "breaks milk" (lets loose of some
milk) when squeezed.

Add an optional shake of cinnamon and nutmeg.
Melt butter in a large oblong pan. Pour in bread
pudding. Bake at 350 degrees for 45 minutes.

Hard Sauce:

1 stick (½ c.) butter
1 egg
1 c. sugar
1-3 t. flavoring (vanilla, rum, or brandy)
(Or you can use ¼ c. of real rum, whiskey, or brandy. Alcohol will evaporate.)

Melt butter in a medium-sized saucepan; add sugar. Mix a small amount of water with a beaten egg in a small bowl; stir some of the hot, melted sugar and butter into this bowl. Beat. Slowly add this egg-butter-sugar mixture to rest of the butter-sugar mixture in the saucepan. Cook until it coats a wooden spoon. Add flavoring last, heating about 30 seconds to one minute. Ladle warm sauce over individual servings of bread pudding.

Becky's Low-Cal Fruit Sauce Alternative:

Blend a can of fruit (any size, any fruit or fruit mix) or fresh/frozen fruit (add a little water) in a blender. Pour in a bowl or pan and sweeten, if needed, to taste. (I like to use fruit in natural fruit juice and then I add Sucanat, date sugar, or brown sugar.) Add a bit of butter or butter substitute, vanilla, or other flavoring.

This can be used as a fruit sauce for any number of recipes or served over ice cream or my favorite way—served warm in a bowl with a dab of sour cream. I call it Fruit Soup and love it on wintry days when I want something sweet, but fairly nourishing!

10

"Wanna Grill Some Burgers?"

Guy Friends

I never had a big brother, and from the time I was small I can remember envying other girls who had them. I had a younger brother, who I love very much, but as the Big Sister, I always felt more maternal toward David and our younger sister, Rachel. My self-assigned role in the family was to look out for them and not so much the other way around. (Although in later years, I've unburdened myself enough to my little sister for her to earn the role of Most Maternal Sibling, at least part-time.)

Rather shy for most of my growing-up years, I was especially nervous around boys. They liked football and worms and dirt and stuff. Though I was intrigued with their otherness, and often admired the cute ones from way across the schoolroom—frankly, they made me sweat. In fact, that was my first clue that I was probably in love with Scott at age 15. He was the only boy I could be myself with, and he never made me sweat. (Not that he didn't make my heart skip a beat or two, but I never remember being anything but completely comfortable around Scott Freeman—even two years before we were an official "item.")

Since Scott and I began dating seriously at 15 and 16, and I married him at age 17—going from my yellow-checked gingham, girlhood bedroom straight to a honeymoon suite—I didn't have much of a chance to get to knows guys as good buddies. Going steady with a guy usually puts other boys at bay, and going to college as a married lady, taking all my classes with Scott, turned me into a walking No Boys Allowed sandwich board.

Boys-turned-men (especially those around my own age) continued to make me sweat if I were left alone with one of their species for more than five minutes. What would I say to a man, other than Scott? "How 'bout them Cowboys?" "You wanna go kick some tires?" The whole man/woman friendship idea seemed as foreign to me as talking to aliens. (Maybe men ARE from Mars.)

But as great as girlfriends are, and as much as I love and cherish my own husband—can we *talk?*—I've come to discover there are times when nothing but a good, brotherly guy friend will do. Both Scott and I would have missed so much without the friends we enjoy who hail from different gender planets. Obviously, there are risks when you talk about friendships with the other gender. After all, almost all affairs begin with an innocent friendship. But within careful boundaries (see my chapter, "We're Just Friends. Warning! Warning!" in *Chocolate Chili Pepper Love*) women can enjoy a nice range of guy friends who sometimes rate right up there with a great girlfriend.

For example, I think everyone needs one guy friend who can make you laugh out loud on a really bad day. The Class Clown that never completely resigned from the job. The guy that makes coming to work slightly less painful for everybody in the office because he knows just the right off-the-wall comment to break the tension of a much-too-long meeting.

One of my favorite funny guy friends is Chip MacGregor, actor/musician turned pastor turned professor turned editor turned literary agent. (Okay, so he has a short attention span.) Any writer who has received one of his famous, hilarious responses to serious questions has laughed out loud and then immediately asked themselves, "Why is this guy not writing humor for good money?" My only guess is that Chip must enjoy the immediate response from his e-buddies, and he uses our questions as fodder for his slightly-off-kilter responses.

I have gathered, over the last few years, a nice stack of "E-Quips from Chip"—sometimes passing them on to friends who love to laugh—and, trust me, I've thought of stealing his stuff and calling it my own. As an example for you, I think I'll just share Chip's hot-off-the computer latest, fresh from this morning.

I wrote Chip today that I needed his advice. Chip used to produce something like 10,000 pages of copy a day to keep his family alive on a poor writer's salary. In the process he became something of a writing machine. A phenomenon. Now I happen to be really behind on this very manuscript. It's due in a week and a half, and I've already asked for one extension due to that broken right arm. (I mean, I could be wrong but I think this excuse comes under Legitimate Reasons to Adjust Contract. Right next to Act of God or Act of Nature. Or in my case, Act of Natural Stupidity.)

"So, Chip, ol' buddy, ol' pal," I wrote, "any recommendations for whipping out wonderful prose in an unbelievably ridiculous amount of time?"

His answer came back within seconds, just to show you how fast this guy thinks on his feet. (Or I guess when we're talking about computer people, it's more like "thinks in his seat." But that doesn't really sound right either.)

> Okay, Becky, as for the writing miracle, here's my advice: copy something from somebody else's book. Maybe a Mark Twain book, who everybody likes but nobody reads any more. It always worked for me. OR you could try getting on the phone and faking a bad cold, being whiny and insisting you need one extra week. (That worked for me too, but I had to really practice my coughs.) Maybe you could invite your sister Rachel to write it for you—she's not doing anything, and the baby's already here, so she doesn't have to worry anymore, right? One last thought: turn in a disk with nothing but squizzles and boxes on it, then blame their computer people for ruining your work. By the time they get it all figured out, you'll have time to write the rest of the book!
>
> As you can see, I'm chock full of good ideas. Any more and I'd have to charge you a consulting fee.
>
> Yours,
>
> Chip

Then there's the thinker. The guy friend who is thoughtful and deep. The sort of man that makes you want to ask, poignantly, "Okay, what IS the meaning of life?" Because the result will be a rich and stimulating conversation, though you know, in the end, you'll only get a mysterious, meandering answer that only leads to more questions. But it's the conversation process and not the product that makes this kind of friend so much fun.

It helps if this insightful guy friend has been through some of life's inevitable wounding, for it gives him a certain tenderness and compassion around the eyes to temper the bane of a bright mind—pride.

This guy friend for me is Lee Hough, a gracious but exacting editor I've been privileged to work with on a couple of manuscript projects. Not my own books, but books belonging to my clients during those days when I did a pretty fair impersonation of an agent. And though I tease him about being too serious, too picky, and in great need of quitting early and going out for a dip cone at Dairy Queen, I think Lee is one of the finest editors I've ever known.

To be candid, I'd be worried about writing for him, because of this very fact—could I withstand the scrutiny? And because I value our friendship apart from the author/editor relationship. He CARES, and cares passionately, about the projects under his editorial wings. If he's tough, it's because he doesn't want his name associated with a book that isn't gut-wrenchingly honest, filled with heart-touching (but non-sappy) stories. He only wants to midwife (midhusband?) books that are relevant to readers who live in the real world where the Christian path doesn't always feel like "the wonderful plan God has for your life"—a reality so many walking wounded understand all too well. Like his own agonizing experience of watching his 20-year marriage dissolve into divorce—no matter how excruciatingly hard he tried to make it work, no matter how many years he prayed for a miracle to mend the broken pieces.

Most of us have some area of our life that baffles our faith, if we're really honest, and Lee has a subtle way of forcing his friends to be just that.

It is probably why Ken Gire, a mutual friend and best-selling author, dedicated his book *Windows of the Soul* to

Lee, writing, "To Lee Hough, my wish for every man is a friend as good as he."

Most of my communication within my little circle of friends includes lots of self-deprecating humor, but Lee doesn't follow my wacky lead in the way he treats me. In fact, to my surprise and honor, he treats me as an intellectual equal (as often as I try to explain to him that I'm just a psuedo-intellectual, faking it from years of mimicking my father, who is the real philosophical brain in our family).

He tells me I'm insightful and have great ideas. He asks my opinion just as easily as if I were a member of his editorial team. Recently he even asked me if he could hire me to come up with some titles for a couple of book projects because, "you're the best title person I know." Lee probably had no idea what this gesture meant to me; how it made me feel smart, and reminded me that maybe I really am—just a little bit.

In observing Lee in all sorts of situations, even as the tough editor delivering hard-to-take criticism, I've always seen him treat women as sisters and as ladies. Not that he doesn't succumb to relaxed, even riotous, laughter in the company of women friends. (Several of us recently observed Lee perform at a publishing banquet in a crazy skit where he busted up a perfectly good guitar.) But there's a certain benevolent, gentlemanly kindness hovering about him that at once makes you feel safe and treasured.

I would echo Ken's heart, and wish for every woman one guy friend as good as he.

And then there's the big brotherly friend—the golden retriever of guy friends—loyal and protective and advising. Bob Briner was this to me, and I missed him sorely during the first year after his death. It wasn't even like we talked often; there were months between notes and calls. But I knew he was there if ever I did need a big brother. And that mattered and meant the world to me.

A few years ago, I had a disappointing experience with a male literary agent, mostly because I felt like a little girl in a man's world when I was around him. He probably didn't even realize it, but I always felt as if he was secretly wanting to say, "Now, Honey, just leave the thinking to me." I felt an enormous sense of freedom when I got out of that contract and determined to shop my manuscripts solo or work only with a female agent in the future.

Then, via the encouragement of AttaGirlfriend, Cheri Fuller, I met Greg Johnson. And it was—how should I say this?—*comfort* at first sight. He had my husband's relaxed, non-pressured air about him—as if the furthest thing from his mind was to be pushy. One of Greg's clients calls him Opie, and, in truth, he does look like a basketball-player-sized version of Andy Griffith's son. Very unintimidating. Add to Opie's looks a laid-back John-Boy Walton personality and there you have it: a Greg.

I knew Cheri was verbal, like me, and creative, like me, and it gave me hope that if Greg could enjoy long-term relationships with other hyper-creative women-types who could spit out three brilliant book ideas in one day, then trash them all the next, well, maybe, just maybe, he could stand being my agent.

Still, I felt I had to issue a warning: "Greg, I'm probably high maintenance to some extent. Not that I'm argumentative or hard to please, but I'm verbal, I like to brainstorm. I NEED to feel like I can do that with an agent without holding back. I have to be able to tell you exactly what I really feel, and that's hard for me, a recovering people pleaser."

"I like creative people. It's why I love this job," he said with a little shrug.

"But I could be trouble."

"I think I can handle you."

"Okay, then—it's a deal."

And it was. Such a deal.

Greg's classic sign-off to me (and I assume his other female clients) is "I love serving you, sister." He not only encouraged my brainstorming, he prayed for us daily during a difficult time with our son and always pointed me to do the right thing even when it was hard: in relationships with others, and in keeping family priorities above tempting offers. I know, from chatting with his other women clients (we secretly call ourselves his literary harem), that Greg makes each of us feel as if we are the only client he has.

When one of my books didn't exactly fly out of the shoot in terms of sales, a book I'd put 150 percent of my efforts and hopes into, Greg called to check on me, knowing I was hurting.

I answered the phone with a lump in my throat, my nose red from snorting and crying. All he said was, "Oh, sister..." and my heart melted. Then he assured me, as he has many times since, that he didn't want to be my agent because he needed the bucks. (I can't help but wonder if it was because he needed the laughs...) "I'm really a shepherd at heart," he said, "and if I weren't an agent, I'd probably be a pastor. I love your writing, I love serving you."

"But what if I never have a book that sells great? I can't take the pressure of this feeling that I have to become some-thing 'big'—to be somebody besides who I am today, just a mom in the country who likes to write and tell stories."

"Who's pressuring you?" he asked gently.

"I guess I am pressuring myself," I finally replied.

"Then relax and write from your heart."

"Is it okay if we don't try to sell big books for big bucks?" I asked through my pitiful tears. "Can we just look for a nice publisher that gives really nice parties at the booksellers' convention and makes me feel loved and likes my work—and forget the prestige of the super-sized publishing houses for now?"

"You bet."

"So I can just write for fun."

"Yep."

"And that's really okay with you?"

"Absolutely."

And we hung up the phone having crossed the line from agent/client to friend/friend. (And that's why I'm writing this book for the most wonderful publishing house that treats me like a member of the family and gives the most amazing parties at the convention every year.)

Speaking of the convention, this past summer in New Orleans, I thought I'd escaped my Annual CBA Breakdown. I had an absolute ball with all my writing girlfriends, as well as some fun events with the "guy friends." Publishers had been super to me, interviewers were generous, and fans had stood in long lines for my books. The AttaGirl brunch had gone well. But somewhere between packing my suitcase and struggling to the airport with a broken, bruised right arm, now throbbing in pain, and being searched at the security gate, and being told that the airplane home was over-booked, exhaustion took control of my good senses, and I just flat lost it. Sat down, folded my battered, broken, bruised arm over my good arm, which was holding my useless plane ticket, and boo-hooed my heart out. Before long, the stewardess came over and bribed me to stop crying by offering to give me a $400.00 voucher and a seat on the next plane that would leave within the hour.

Funny how a $400.00 voucher can just perk you right up. Almost immediately I started feeling a whole lot better.

I looked around the empty airport and smiling to myself, remembered that other convention where I had tried to escape to a quiet back alley for my breakdown only to have Bob Briner appear out of nowhere, like a big brotherly guardian angel. And my heart hurt a little.

Lord, who will be Bob in my life now?

Then the most ordinary, remarkable thing happened.

I looked up from where I was sitting, having asked that question half-wondering, half-conversing with God. I was still a little glassy-eyed from the latest tearletting, but through the mistiness of spent emotion, I could see that sitting across from me was none other than Greg Johnson. Nobody else around us. Just Greg, having silently, miraculously appeared out of nowhere, sitting there with the casual friendliness of a faithful retriever, smiling his big Opie smile.

"Want a bite of my sandwich?" he offered, his own mouth stuffed with pastrami on wheat.

I smiled and shook my head, then asked him if he would guard my suitcase while I went to the restroom and powdered my face. (A face that, Lord knows, needed a lot more than powder to salvage it at that point!)

I made it to just inside the door before a new flood of tears accompanied a prayer of profound gratitude. I couldn't help wondering if the Lord allowed Bob in on this uncanny moment at the airport departure gate. I could easily imagine the Tubby Texan telling God, "Look, this gal is obviously going to need some help down there. I think Greg Johnson might be just the guy for the job. Why don't you send him on over with a pastrami on wheat and a big friendly smile?"

Sometimes girlfriends are all we need. But there are those moments, those wonderful moments, when nothing but a good ol' guy friend will do.

There is a friend who sticks closer than a brother.
PROVERBS 18:24

"A listening ear, a supportive comment, a caring heart touches an ache within that continuing on responsibly doesn't quite relieve. We value the encouragement that occurs when something uniquely human comes out of another person and into us."
—Dr. Larry Crabb, *Hope When You're Hurting*

Girlfriend's Guy-Translation Dictionary

"I'M GOING FISHING."

Translated: "I'm going to stand by a stream with a stick in my hand, while the fish swim by in complete safety."

"CAN I HELP WITH DINNER?"

Translated: "Why isn't it already on the table?"

"UH-HUH," "SURE, HONEY," OR "YES, DEAR."
Translated: Absolutely nothing. It's a conditioned response.

"IT WOULD TAKE TOO LONG TO EXPLAIN."
Translated: "I have no idea how it works."

"TAKE A BREAK, HONEY, YOU'RE WORKING TOO HARD."
Translated: "I can't hear the game over the vacuum cleaner."

"THAT'S INTERESTING, DEAR."
Translated: "Are you still talking?"

"YOU KNOW HOW BAD MY MEMORY IS."
Translated: "I remember the theme song to 'F Troop,' the address of the first girl I ever kissed, and the vehicle identification numbers of every car I've ever owned...but I forgot your birthday."

"OH, DON'T FUSS, I JUST CUT MYSELF, IT'S NO BIG DEAL."
Translated: "I have actually severed a limb, but will bleed to death before I admit that I'm hurt."

"I CAN'T FIND IT."
Translated: "It didn't fall into my outstretched hands, so I'm completely clueless."

"WHAT DID I DO THIS TIME?"
Translated: "What did you catch me at?"

"YOU KNOW I COULD NEVER LOVE
ANYONE ELSE."

Translated: "I am used to the way you yell at
me, and realize it could be worse."

"YOU LOOK TERRIFIC."

Translated: "I'm begging you, please, don't try
on one more outfit, I'm starving."

"I'M NOT LOST. I KNOW EXACTLY
WHERE WE ARE."

Translated: "No one will ever see us alive again."

Chip's Recipe for a Macho Guy Meal

The following is "Chip's recipe for guys on a Saturday afternoon watching the University of Oregon Ducks." (Author note: I had to admit, I fell over laughing when I found out there is a real football team called the Fighting Ducks! But let's keep that little secret between us girls, okay?)

1. Appetizer: open bag of Doritos.

2. Salad course: cut a tomato for the burger.

3. Soup course: open canned, cold beverage—your choice (if you want soup, add "Place cold canned beverage in sun for 40 minutes").

4. Main course: big juicy hunk of dead cow.

5. Pasta course: if the dead cow is ground up, put it on a burger with ketchup, pickles, onions, and cheese...if it's just a big hunk of dead cow, eat it with a baked potato.

6. To Cleanse the Palate: open another bag of Doritos. Drink with chilled canned beverage.

7. Vegetables: Aren't Doritos made of corn?

8. Dessert: Ice cream eaten with spoon straight out of carton. Maybe also need a cold canned beverage, with bubbles in it, to wash the ice cream down.

11

"You're My Best Friend in the Whole World"

Hubby Friend

For a middle-aged mother of four, this is an ADVENTURE. I'm on a plane that just took off from Dallas-Ft. Worth, heading to a remote island in the Caribbean. Scott is beside me dressed in khaki shorts, a Hawaiian shirt, Teva sandals, and topped off with an Aussie Outback-style leather hat. Oh, and he also brought his fishing pole aboard. Typical of my husband, he is fully INTO anything smacking of outdoorsmen thrills: lock, stock and rod & reel. He's intensely absorbed in an issue of *Dive* magazine, occasionally stopping to show me a picture of tropical fishies, excited as a boy let out of school. He plans to become Scott Cousteau by week's end, I can tell.

I'm seeing glimpses again of the boy I fell in love with when I was a young girl of 15. After nearly a quarter century of babies, teens, bills, and jobs, it's easy to forget that my husband is not just a father to our kids and payer of bills, but my very best friend.

Our marriage needs a chance to remember that again. How long has it been since we embarked on a getaway— spent a few days just playing together?

We are en route to a small island in the Caymans because a kind-hearted, soft-spoken woman named Mary Brandis, whose family owns much of the property on Cayman Brac and Little Cayman, asked me to speak at a women's retreat. (She's calling it *Barefoot and Breaking Free* and is putting on this event as a gift to herself and to her friends, after what has been a very tough year.) She's ready to run free in the sand again, abandon herself to her Lord anew. Mary has invited between 50 and 75 American women, and the same number of islanders, to the Brac Reef Resort she owns and manages.

Scott, usually reluctant to accompany me to "ladies' things," took no time in offering himself as companion and bag carrier to "sacrifice for Jesus in the Caymans."

Yesterday, Mary called me at home from the resort as I was frantically searching for birth certificates to get Scott and me safely across the border. "I've found Scott's," I told her, "but mine seems to be missing. But, hey, here's a marriage license—I'll toss that in just in case I can piggyback on his birth certificate by virtue of being legally married to him."

"Why don't you just keep looking for that birth certificate," Mary said with a laugh.

Minutes later, I hung up the phone and—voila!—found my birth certificate. Now we could prove I was born, without my having to drag my mother to the airport and having her show them her stretch marks. RELIEF.

But a funny thing happened today as we stood at the airline counter to purchase our tickets. "May I see your birth certificates?" the attendant asked.

"Sure," I said handing her the documents.

"Pardon me," she countered, directing her comments to Scott. "But this birth certificate does not match your driver's license. It says, 'Ezekiel Scott Freeman.' Are you Ezekiel?"

"No," Scott said, panic showing in his bulging eyes. "That would be my son." Then he turned to me. "Honeeeey, didn't you say not to worry, that you had my birth certificate?" I knew he was contemplating the scenario of his being left behind on a 105-degree August day in Texas, waving to me as I took off—alone—for cool island breezes.

I looked at the lady helplessly. "I must have accidentally grabbed my son's birth certificate instead of my husband's." With palms up, I shrugged toward Scott, who was now holding his head in his hands, and cheerfully added, "Whoops." It did not help.

A young man approached the counter to try to help. "Do you, by any chance, have your marriage license with you?" he asked.

Scott rolled his eyes and started to say, "Fat chance..." as I produced the needed document with the flourish of a magician. Indeed, he looked at me as if I'd just pulled a live rabbit out of my totebag.

Since I enjoy staying a bit of a mystery to my husband, the only explanation I offered was a wide grin.

We've all heard jokes about "island time," so perhaps Scott and I should not be surprised that the pilot just announced—mid-air—that our connecting flight from Grand Cayman to Cayman Brac will be a bit delayed; he estimates about a four-hour wait.

I look at Scott and point to the Cayman Air insignia on the leaflet in front of us. "Well, what can we expect from an airline whose symbol is a peg-leg turtle?"

He laughs and we snuggle like sleepy kids, my head on his lap, as we wait for the landing, and the next plane that will take us to Paradise.

I cannot believe it's been five days since we deboarded the peg-leg plane and were swallowed up by paradise.

I've had what feels like a month of experiences. Scott's been more free to roam and play; and though I'm tired and hungering for solitude now, I've had an incredible time with the retreatees!

Mary's dream—to help other women renew their joy and freedom—was fulfilled this weekend in ways beyond ourselves. Last night we stuffed a huge bottle with small slips of paper upon which we'd written all our heartaches and emotional burdens. Then together we heave-hoed the bottle out into the dark waves of the blue-green sea. "I'll cast all my cares upon you, I'll lay all my burdens down at Your feet," we sang through tear-filled eyes as we watched the bottle ebb and flow away, away, away—under the benediction of a perfect, luminescent moon.

A perfect ending to Part One (Serving Others) of this island experience.

▲ ▼ ▲ ▼ ▲

Part Two (Vegging Out) begins today with the pleasure of solitude, the sand, and the sea. In a couple of hours, when Mr. Scott Cousteau returns from sea fishing, I'll also enjoy the pleasure of some romantic time alone with him. The peg-leg turtle plane came early this morning and whisked everyone else away. The resort is nearly deserted during this off-season week, and I am luxuriating in this precious moment of quiet.

Right now (even I can hardly believe it!) I'm lying in a wide, white-roped hammock under a thatched roof. (There's even a little rope hanging down from the rafters with a handle on it that I can pull when I want to make the hammock swing. Rock-a-bye me.) The breeze coming off the prettiest water I've ever seen is a perfect 70 degrees. The ocean shimmering before me is sparkling its clear jewel-toned shades of bright blue and brilliant aqua. The whole scene is picturesquely framed by green coconut palms swaying in the breeze. Clouds appear to rise out of the ocean's edge—like fluffy Dr. Seuss mountains of white.

Today I'm on the island of Little Cayman, even smaller and less populated (200 people) than Cayman Brac—having been carried to shore by Mr. T, Mary's 77-year-old father, late yesterday afternoon. Well, actually, Mr. Tibbets allowed *me* to drive his glass-bottomed boat while he entertained me with stories from his island days of yore: the hurricane of '32 that swept away his grandmother, his 19-year-old sister and his baby brother; how, as a boy, he'd row a little boat out to meet the big sailing ships; and the day he jumped on that sailing ship to seek his fortune. Amazingly, he found it—in lumber and now owns a fleet of lumber stores across Florida and these islands.

Scott and I marvel at the energy of this man who rises with the sun and goes to bed only after everyone else gives up in exhaustion. (Is it the island air he's breathed all his life? The pounds of cod oil he's ingested?) As we sailed along the brilliant blue sea, watching flying fish leap forth as we zipped near them, I looked up at Scott from under my native-made straw hat as I sat proudly steering the boat from the captain's chair. "Can you believe we are really doing this?"

Scott just smiled broadly in reply, shaking his head in equal wonder.

We were two kids, free, sailing away into the blue.

I did it!

Yesterday I donned a pair of hot-pink flippers and an equally eye-catching snorkel and mask, and waddled into the clear cool edge of the sea holding on as best I could to Scott's steadying hand. He patiently instructed me on how to breathe through the snorkel tube, but when I first put my masked face underwater, my body responded with claustrophobia and panic—it seemed so unhuman to breathe underwater and I immediately missed the use of my nostrils for inhaling air. But Scott assured me I would adjust. He ducked his mask underwater, then came up, lifted his mask on his head, and grinned. "Trust me, Babe, you don't want to miss this!"

Down I went again, relaxing as Scott—the protector—held my hand and reassured me all was well. I could not believe my eyes! I suddenly forgot everything around me, caught up with the curiosity of an alien exploring another planet. The water was clear as smooth glass—200 feet visibility! As I swam softly through the underwater world of silence, I realized God had been having an awfully good time Under de Sea, where human eyes seldom explore. I might as well have been swimming in a giant tropical aquarium—brilliant coral, angelfish, trumpet fish, starfish, tarpon, barracuda, sea turtles, stingrays, clownfish, blowfish, lobster, and tiny little fishes in colors one usually only sees on teenagers' neon-dyed hair. I've seen so many beautiful sights in my life that I thought I was beyond being surprised. But I literally teared up at the sight of the enveloping beauty, wetting my mask from the inside out. Scott swam over to me, pointing and gliding, taking me to places I'd never dreamed of going.

When our play time was over, we plodded together out of the ocean, like some emerging sea monsters—our frog-like fins criss-crossing now and then. We laughed so hard I nearly fell backwards, but Scott caught me in his able arm before I hit sand and pulled me to him.

"Becky," he said quietly.

"What?" I asked.

"I was just thinking."

"What is it?" I asked again in a near whisper.

"I was just thinking I never thought I would feel this way again. About life, about us. On this island I've caught a glimpse of what almost feels like joy again."

I reached up and kissed this man I love. Prone to melancholy without reminders of fun, adventure, escape, and romance, he can lose his smile. I rarely lose my smile, but I easily lose my head by too much doing, and not enough BEING.

How grand that we re-discovered relaxed joy together.

Tonight we fell easily into bed and into each other's arms like the newlyweds we once were, the friends and lovers we find we still are. After all these years, and kids and fights and making ups—he's still the one.

Before we fall asleep in each other's arms, I read aloud a line from a poem tucked under a candle on the bedside table. "Once you've slept on an island, you'll never be quite the same."

Scott nods and relaxes into the deep sleep of a child. I watch his incredibly handsome face in the glow of the moonlight streaming through the open window. A gentle breeze rocks the palm leaves goodnight.

I am more at peace than I've been in months.

Our last day in Paradise.

Yesterday we took a small plane—a VERY small plane, the sort one frequently sees crashing in jungle movies—from

158 Coffee Cup Friendship and Cheesecake Fun

Little Cayman back to Cayman Brac. Mary and her husband, Russ, left us the keys to their car, which we drove around the Brac on its one road all afternoon.

As we drove and chatted, Scott and I wondered how much marriage counseling we could have saved ourselves through the years if we had played more. Perhaps all we needed, all we've ever really needed, was an occasional week alone on an island playing together.

We explored caves filled with bats (where Scott, the rock climber, scaled every available nook and cranny); stopped for lunch at the bakery and ate some of our favorite local meat patties (a spicy ground beef wrapped and baked like a turnover in orange-colored bread); and drove up to the very tip-top of the cliffs on the north side of the island. This is where a local Caymanian jewelry maker told us we could find some Caymanite—a beautiful semi-precious stone.

At this piece of information Scott's eyes lit up. Before my eyes he transformed from Cousteau, explorer of the seas, to Indiana Jones in search of lost treasure.

Indeed, Scott had found his treasure on a rock-climbing trip in and around the cliffs the day before: several hunks of precious Caymanite.

Now, today, Scott wanted to drive to the cliff to show me the panoramic view of the island and the sea below. As we were standing on the cliff and looking down, 150 feet to the crashing waves below, Scott tossed the camera to me and said, "Take my picture!"

To my horror, when I looked up, my husband was hanging—HANGING—by his fingertips from the rocky ledge. One false move and it would be the last picture I ever had of Scott alive. I wanted to strangle him. I wanted to faint. My legs turned to jelly and my stomach turned upside down. But I was afraid if I argued he'd get distracted and lose his grip. So I snapped the picture and slowly put the camera down and walked toward the car—too frightened to speak or look back. Once he was safe, he ran alongside me asking, "What's the matter, Babe?" I thought I would throw up—my head pounded with a fury. By the time we reached the car, I was crying the sort of tears mothers cry after they've found a small child they thought had been kidnapped.

"I know you thought you were safe," I sobbed, "but let me just say this one thing: Don't ever ask me to take a picture of you hanging off a 150-foot cliff again. I thought you were going to die—and just when I almost got you the way that I wah-wah-want you after all these years!"

At least my beloved isn't boring. And I will never question his manhood. His common sense, perhaps, but never his machismo.

▲ ▼ ▲ ▼ ▲

Now we're flying home—to faxes, traffic jams, deadlines, and laundry piles. I dread the re-entry into reality, I have to admit, but I miss my children and my Texas friends. Scott, who draws his breath from nature's beauty, is especially sullen about returning to the dry flatlands of Texas.

Beautiful caramel-skinned flight attendants are offering us coffee, tea, soft drinks, or rum punch. We wave good-bye to the islands shrinking below us as if they're friends, which they are, sort of. We carry back coconuts, a bit of precious Caymanite, and a conch shell the size of a small watermelon, which smells by now, I am sure, like a small rotting dumpster in our suitcase. (Last night I was lying blissfully in the hotel bed when I heard what sounded like a rock tumbler— whack-whack-WHACK—issuing from the bathroom. "What's happening?" I'd shouted. "Go back to sleep," Scott had replied, panting heavily, "I'm just killing a conch!")

What else do we carry with us? Memories of salt-tinged breezes on moonlit nights. A passionate kiss, stolen in an island cave. Shared glimpses of the marvels of the sea and everything that walks around it, flies above it, and swims under it.

And that old feeling for each other we'd almost forgotten, and vow never to forget again.

After all, we've slept on an island now—and we'll never be quite the same again.

How many are your works, O LORD! In wisdom you
made them all....There is the sea, vast and spacious,
teeming with creatures beyond number—living things
both large and small. There the ships go to and fro,
and the leviathan, which you formed to frolic there.
These all look to you...
PSALM 104:24-27

"How wonderful are islands! Existence
in the present gives island living an extreme
vividness and purity. One lives like a child or
a saint in the immediacy of here and now."
—Anne Morrow Lindbergh, *Gift from the Sea*

Is Your Husband/Wife Friendship "Oceanic"?

Dr. Paul Ka'ikena Pearsall is a clinical psychologist who has spent his life in the Polynesian culture, studying interactions between the brain, mind, body, and immune system. He believes there is Eastern Thought, Western Thought, and a third way of looking at life and love, which he deems may be healthiest of all: Island Thought.

Whether or not we agree with the basic philosophy of the culture, there's much we go-go-go Westerners can learn from those who were raised on island time.

Here are some quotes from wise, esteemed islanders on the subject of relationships taken from Dr. Pearsall's book, *The Pleasure Prescription*.[8]

"Love is...how you treat a person, not just how you feel about a person....Once you learn to do loving, loving is forever. It takes many, many years to learn how to love someone, so you must be persistently patient with your partner and with yourself. If you think you are falling out of love, you are getting love lazy and not doing enough real loving. Only very patient persons should marry, because lasting love is very hard work for a very long time. Anyone can fall in love, but staying in love is a way of daily life led between two persons."

"If you put your partner down, that is exactly where they will stay and how they will feel. Always try to put your partner up, make him or her feel very good, and try to make their life better because they are with you."

"Westerners speak of codependence as an illness, but we see it as the ultimate healthy way to relate. Every relationship should be codependent, with each person taking care of the other, trying to please the other and protecting the other."

"My husband and I see our marriage as our most treasured gift. We are so lucky to be together and to have one another to remind us about the sunsets and sunrises, that we would never do anything to ruin that gift. Without each other, there could be no pleasure." (Quoted from a Hawaiian couple, married 57 years.)

Island Rice Pudding

2 cups cooked brown rice (I cook up brown rice in big batches, then freeze for using in dishes like this one! The instant brown rice can be used in a pinch—sure is faster and easier, though not as nutritious as the time consuming, pot-watching kind!)

2 cup milk, soy milk or rice milk

½ c. raisins

½ c. brown sugar, Sucanat or date sugar

½ c. unsweetened coconut (if you use sweetened coconut, cut back on the sugar)

2 strips of orange peel

dash salt

1 T. butter or a few butter sprays

1 t. vanilla

dash cinnamon or nutmeg, if you like

Mix all ingredients together (except vanilla). Cook over medium heat until thickened. (This takes at least 10 - 20 minutes.) Remove orange peel and add vanilla. Serve warm or cold. (In winter, I love this warm. In summer, it's more refreshing to eat chilled.)

Part V

▲ ▼ ▲

Kindred Spirits &
Big Bosom Buddies

Experiences That Connect Us
Heart to Heart

12

"She Has Your Eyes, Mom"

Mother/Daughter Friends

There's something about holding your own newborn child and experiencing the tidal wave of love sweep over your heart that gives you a whole new appreciation for your own mother. Because you now realize that a younger version of your own mother, not so long ago, was holding you in her arms, overwhelmed with unspeakable love. Our mothers and mothers-in-law are generally the only two women on the planet who love our children, their grandbabies, as much as we do.

If you happen to have had a close sister or two—proud aunties—welcoming the new baby, you probably had an experience of female bonding so strong you could almost see the estrogen dripping off everyone's chin.

I just returned from one such Estrogen Baby-Bonding experience among three generations of females in my family. No, I've not given birth since we last visited by book. However, someone very close to me has just blessed our family with a new addition.

Maybe I should back up and begin at the beginning.

The last two years were some of the most difficult years my sister, Rachel, has ever passed through. Even if you've not read of her meticulous, things-under-control personality in my past books, you've now read of her detail (albeit funny!) orientation in this volume.

Rachel lived a pretty halcyon existence in a nice, neat Virginia neighborhood, with a nice, neat husband with a nice, neat job and together they raised one nice, neat child, Trevor. She drove every morning to a nice, neat coffee shop and upon the first sip of her steaming latté would say a prayer of thanks for her nice, neat life. And then her nice, neat husband lost his nice, neat job to a nasty, messy corporate take-over.

And that's when the threads of all-she'd-once-counted-on began unwinding, one by one.

After a year of job searching in a too-crowded field, my sister and her little family had to sell their home and store everything that had given her surroundings familiarity. With heart-breaking resignation, they had to move from beautiful Virginia to the flatlands of Texas to live with our parents for a few months, while her husband continued the search for work. E-mails from Rachel during that period were especially poignant. My funny sister was hurting, and I ached along with her.

One day she wrote, "You know, Beck, sometimes I wonder if down the road I'll be glad in a sad kind of way about all we've been through. For example, let's just say that you help me get a book contract and we sell billions and billions of copies. To be honest with you (and I'm tearing up as I contemplate this), I'm not sure I would ever look back

and say, 'O.K., this was worth going through that.' Do you
know what I mean? I feel at this moment that I will always
look back on this time as very painful, demoralizing, and
scary. Not to say that I won't see the silver linings, but I
guess I feel that when my life is over, I'll just think, *There
were some very special times, but also some very painful
times, and now it's over."*

Thankfully, a reprieve came in the form of freelance work
in Atlanta, but Rachel, like Tigger, had lost her bounce.
When Trevor would try to be tougher than the lump forming
in his throat, and when he'd lose the battle and cry out in
pain for his old life, his old friends, and his old school,
Rachel thought her heart might not bear it.

Some days she'd draw strength from God's Word, some
days she'd feel that He was playing tricks with her hopes.
Some days she didn't have the strength to think or feel at all:
she was doing good to just get up, move slowly and achingly
through the day, and pray that the earthquake that had
wrecked her nice, neat life would soon be over.

Eventually, the freelance assignment took on more permanent proportions and the little family moved to Atlanta to
an apartment that overlooked a comforting lake. As Rachel
began to gather some of her own familiar pots and pans and
pictures into the apartment, and sat by the window and
watched the leaves turn from summer green to rich, fall colors
of orange and red and yellow, hope began to raise its tired
head once again. Small joys—like great writing assignments
and positive comments from editors and our sister get-away
trips—were also helpful. One thing she missed most, however, in this new city, was a friend. We take them for granted
until we have no one to call up and ask to meet us for coffee
and conversation. No one to bring the cheesecake when the
time would come for celebration or commiseration.

So when I came to the Atlanta area for a speaking engagement, I took her under my big sister wing and determined to find her a friend. The first night, as I looked out at an audience of about 1,000 friendly, Southern-style women, I introduced Rachel to them and said, "My little sister here has just moved to Atlanta, and we'd like to announce that she needs a couple of girlfriends. Preferably friends who are witty and relaxed and a little artsy—with a young son for her seven-year-old son to play with. If you'd like to candidate to be my sister's new best friend, just meet her at the book table and we'll talk."

We all laughed—the audience, Rachel, and I. Then I dove into my talk—funny stories mostly—and then I chatted my way to the poignant section of my speech. At this point, I noticed Rachel covering her mouth and exiting from the back. There were snickers here and there, like random kernels popping, in the audience. Not knowing what to do—whether I'd hurt Rachel's feelings or said something funny—I just plowed on through to the finish line.

After the talk, I immediately found Rachel and asked her, "What was up with the leaving?"

"Becky," she said, struggling to control her emotions—of sadness or hilarity I couldn't yet tell. "Becky," she began again, "while you were speaking so seriously, the big screen that magnified your face malfunctioned and above your head, in giant red letters, the words, 'Warning! Warning!' began blinking. I'm sorry, but I just couldn't stop laughing. I had to get out of there and get some fresh air to gain control again."

It was good to see my sister laughing so hard, even if it had to be at my expense. (And might I add that my announcement yielded two strong prospects that have since become Rachel's new Atlanta girlfriends!)

Later that night, we bundled up in my rental car and drove to a local café. "So how are things going?" I inquired sincerely. "Are you feeling all right? You didn't eat much tonight."

"I know," she said slowly. "I think I might be just a little bit pregnant. I'm so out of control of the universe now that I can't even get my birth control under control."

And so, as it turned out, she was more than a little bit pregnant. Eight years after giving birth to Trevor, Rachel was once again incubating new life. And though she worried about the timing (how unplanned and off-schedule it all was!), somehow we all knew that this baby was no accident. It was a gift, fresh from the hand of God for her Out of Control, Starting-Over-From-Scratch Life.

This past weekend, I flew to North Carolina to speak at The Cove and then drove up to hold my beautiful newborn niece, Tori Leigh, all seven pounds, seven ounces of miracle-in-the-flesh. Mother had landed in town just a couple of hours before Rachel went into labor and was there in the delivery room when Tori made her grand debut. Mother gave a blow-by-blow (or a push-by-push) account to my father through her cell phone. Later, my father told me, "I didn't think I'd get emotional, but, Becky, when I heard Rachel's baby girl cry over that cell phone, I cried right along with her."

I'd been worried about Mother making the trip to Atlanta—in fact her heart had been acting up a bit before the impending birth of her grandchild. Just before I took off for North Carolina, I called her and said, "Mother, if you need to have surgery or anything, no matter how busy I am, I will halt everything to be with you. I want you to know that I'll move in with you and cook and clean and be your nurse-maid...." But before I could even finish my sentence, Mother answered, with intense feeling behind every word—"Oh, Becky dear, you have no idea how motivating that is for me to stay well." I knew then that my quick-witted mother would be fine. For whatever might be ailing us, humor, along with prayer and friends, always promotes a cure. (One of my favorite sayings among females in our family is, "We may have dysfunctions but we at least have the decency to make them sound entertaining.")

I drove from Asheville to Rachel's apartment in Atlanta on a perfect Sunday morning in September—the first, crisp nips of fall playing about the air. Only pausing to give quick hugs to mother and to Rachel, I walked straight from the front door to the nursery for a peek at our baby. As imagined, she was perfect. Downy dark hair, rosebud lips. Tiny body, moving in dreamy slow motion, wrapped in an antique rose-covered nightie, as the light poured on her from a nearby window. She looked like a Rembrandt painting. Her fingers were outstretched toward the light, her eyes struggling to open wide like a puppy's to take in the Big World. I'd forgotten how precious is a newborn's small warm body—the faint scent of baby oil, the silky softness of their skin touching your cheek.

Mother looked at her two daughters, Rachel and me, and at her new granddaughter—the only girl to arrive in our family since my daughter, Rachel Praise, had been born nearly 17 years ago. Love and joy and a sense of all-rightness surrounded us.

Small, ordinary things—a meal shared, a diaper changed, a baby bath, a game played—all seemed extra special. A new baby in the house adds a certain glow to what could seem mundane. That evening, Trevor and his daddy and my mother asked me to join them in a domino game of 42. It was a rousing fun game, although I admit I was a little distracted by the warmth and snuggling of my niece lying half-awake in my arms as I played my hand. Halfway through the game, Trevor asked, "Um, Aunt Becky. I'd kind of like to win a game now. Would you mind if you be my dad's partner so I can have Granny for mine?" Mother just beamed.

The next day I took everyone out for Mexican food—the first out-of-doors outing with baby along. The conversation was typical for the Arnold girls—poignant observations peppered with out-loud laughter. I told of how I'd lost a big chunk of my tooth just before I'd had to leave town and had to go around begging for help from dentist to dentist to find someone who could see me before closing time.

"What did you say to get them to help you?" Mom asked. But before I could answer, my "wheaty" sister piped up, "Well, Mom, I'm pretty sure Becky probably said, 'Pleath, pleath, can you pleath fixth my tooth!'" As the laughter around the table began to die down, the waitress came up to take my order. I chose something I thought would win the admiration of my health-conscious mother: orange roughy with tomatoes and green onions and avocado slices. I pictured it served Mexican style—simmering on a fajita-type plate surrounded by appropriate garnishes. So did everyone else in the family.

When the actual dish arrived, however, we were all caught off guard. Trevor's eyes grew enormous as he looked from the entrée on the waitress's tray to my eyes and back again, waiting for what I might say about this newly presented predicament. What my meal turned out to be, in actuality, was raw fish (I'm assuming it was orange roughy) chopped up in a tall parfait dish, with the tomatoes, avocado, and green onions layered like fudge, nuts, and whipped cream. It was, by all appearances, a cold fish sundae.

"What's this?" I asked the waitress, trying not to act shocked.

Rachel was quick to supply the answer. She may move slowly in the details category, but she's fast with words. "Beck, looks to me like *this*—is Fish in a Dish."

Trevor chimed in, "Yeah—fish in a dish, Aunt Becky!"

Rachel leaned over to offer, deadpan, yet another word of explanation. "I believe they call it the Dr. Seuss Special."

Sometimes, flanked by my mother and my sister, I feel as though we're a living, breathing sitcom.

Just before I left the funny females in my family tree to fly home to my own brood, I shared one last coffee moment over breakfast with Mother and Rach.

I took a bite of warm cinnamon toast and a swallow of Folgers. "Hey, Rachel, remember how you wanted another boy?"

She nodded.

"I know you've always been kind of a tomboy and I know how much you've enjoyed Trevor and his friends," I said with empathy, "but I couldn't help praying all these years that God would give you a daughter, as well. You'll never really understand how I feel about my own daughter, Rachel, until you've raised a little girl. It's going to give us a whole new common experience to talk about. They're so different from little boys. Both girls and boys bring their own unique blessings to a mother's heart."

"Oh, yes," Mother nodded in agreement. "Becky, did you know that your Rachel sent me a Grandparents' Day Card? It was the cutest thing—we opened it up, and this happy music filled the living room; and she signed it so sweetly."

I smiled. "I didn't know she did it, but I'm not surprised. It's one of the wonderful things about a daughter. They communicate! I'd get one or two Post-It-sized notes from Zeke when he was away for two months of the summer on a mission project. But Rach keeps me up to date. She sent this last night by e-mail, knowing instinctively that I need reassurance that they're okay when I have to be away now and then. And she knows I like to hear little bits and pieces from the home front to keep me connected during weekend speaking engagements."

I unfolded the printout and read,

> Dear Mom,
>
> I sent you a picture of me in bluebonnets. So how's the room service? I had rice cakes on a silver platter for dinner. I went on the barge with Zach and Amanda and got a little sun and caught a fish. Dad and Gabe went on the fishing boat together and Gabe caught a five-pound bass. Dad and Zach were both jealous. We just had a lazy sort of day, although I did clean all of the upstairs really good. I've got to get to bed. I hope you're enjoying yourself. Just think, this is the last time you have to be gone for a long time. We're doing fine here, really. We love you lots. Dad and Gabe said hi.
>
> Love, Rachel

My sister Rachel looked over at her daughter, sucking happily on her miniature fingers—a little doll-baby wrapped in a cloud of soft pink.

"I think I'll keep her," she said, bending over to kiss Tori's downy head. "I've decided a daughter was what I wanted after all."

Mothers of an all-boy clan have lots of benefits and their own brand of rough-and-tumble fun. They get to be the Only Girl in the family, and certainly that's special.

But mothers who have at least one daughter mixed in with their sons will tell you there's nothing quite like a little sugar 'n' spice and everything nice, sprinkled around the snips and snails and puppy-dog tails.

Just before I left, I took pictures of Mother and Rachel and baby Tori. They'll go in a scrapbook, and in about 20 years, Tori will be flipping through the yellowing pages and pointing and oohing and aahing and dreaming of the day when she'll become a mother, like her own mother and Aunt Becky and Granny Ruthie and Nonnie before her.

Because the love and laughter and dreams of the females in our family tree is really what little girls are made of.

> *Many daughters have done well,*
> *but you excel them all.*
> PROVERBS 31:29 NKJV

"*...For the love which from our birth*
Over and around us lies,
Lord of all, to Thee we raise
This our hymn of grateful praise."
(From the hymn "For the Beauty of the Earth,"
words by Folliott S. Pierpont)

I Don't Care How Famous You Are:
I'm STILL Your MOTHER!

PAUL REVERE'S MOTHER: "I don't care where you think you have to go, young man, midnight is past your curfew."

MONA LISA'S MOTHER: "After all that money your father and I spent on braces, that's the biggest smile you can give us?"

COLUMBUS'S MOTHER: "I don't care what you've discovered, you still could have written!"

MICHELANGELO'S MOTHER: "Can't you paint on walls like other children? Do you have any idea how hard it is to get that stuff off the ceiling?"

NAPOLEON'S MOTHER: "All right, if you aren't hiding your report card inside your jacket, take your hand out of there and show me."

ABRAHAM LINCOLN'S MOTHER: "Again with the stovepipe hat? Can't you just wear a baseball cap like the other kids?"

MARY'S MOTHER: "I'm not upset that your lamb followed you to school, but I would like to know how he got a better grade than you."

ALBERT EINSTEIN'S MOTHER: "But it's your senior picture. Can't you do something about your hair? Styling gel, mousse, something...?"

GEORGE WASHINGTON'S MOTHER: "The next time I catch you throwing money across the Potomac, you can kiss your allowance good-bye!"

JONAH'S MOTHER: "That's a nice story. Now tell me where you've really been for the last three days."

THOMAS EDISON'S MOTHER: "Of course I'm proud that you invented the electric light bulb. Now turn it off and get to bed."

Time's Effect on Our Daughters

Age 8:   Looks at herself and sees herself as Cinderella/ Sleeping Beauty.

Age 15: Looks at herself and sees herself as a fat Cinderella /Sleeping Beauty with PMS and Pimples, i.e., UGLY—refuses to go out looking like this.

Age 20: Looks at herself and sees "too fat/too thin, too short/too tall, too straight/too curly"—but decides she's going anyway.

Age 30: Looks at herself and sees "too fat/too thin, too short/too tall, too straight/too curly"—but too busy to fix it so she's going anyway.

Age 40: Looks at herself and sees "too fat/too thin, too short/too tall, too straight/too curly"—but says, "At least I'm clean," and goes anyway.

Age 50: Looks at herself and sees "I am" and goes wherever she wants to.

Age 60: Looks at herself and reminds herself of all the people who can't even see themselves in the mirror anymore. Goes out and conquers the world.

Age 70: Looks at herself and sees wisdom, laughter, and ability, goes out and enjoys life.

Age 80: Doesn't bother to look. Just puts on a purple hat and goes out to have fun.

Mom's Oatmeal Gem Cupcakes

(These are wonderful for breakfast or snacks—a great way to eat your oatmeal!)

1 ½ c. old-fashioned oats
1 large apple, peeled and grated
1 mashed banana
⅓ c. dried fruit—any kind
1 t. vanilla
1 T. brown sugar
¼ c. canola oil
⅓ c. chopped nuts, any kind

Optional:
1 T. grated coconut (sweetened or unsweetened)
1 t. each ground coriander and grated orange peel

Mix all ingredients and let stand ten minutes. Spoon into greased muffin tins mounding each muffin above surface of pan; press firmly with back of spoon until muffin cup is full and slightly rounded. Bake 30 minutes, or until lightly browned. (Note: there is no leavening in this recipe so muffins will not rise.)

13

"You've Gotta Read This!"

Bookworm Friends

I met Hope over seafood linguini, Caesar salad, and two red eyes on a cold rainy night in downtown Chicago. Hope, a print publicist, happened to be in Chicago to visit some magazine editors during the same weekend I would be flying in to do radio interviews. Now those of you who've read my previous books will note what a miracle it is that I flew to Chicago (albeit on a plane), rented a car, followed the map, and negotiated my way through the Windy City all by myself, without a hitch. (For those of you who've not read my previous books, let me just mention that Sarah—Melissa's daughter and Gabe's good friend—told me that this week when the teacher asked the class, "What frightens you the most?" Gabe's hand went up immediately. Without hesitation he replied, "My mother's driving." I kid you not, that very afternoon I backed the van into a telephone pole and put an eight-inch dent in it from top to bottom.)

The plan was that after I checked into my hotel, I would drive downtown where Hope and I would "do dinner."

A couple of hours after my plane arrived, I was running across a Chicago street, my coat wrapped tightly around me, then ducked inside to the warmth of the restaurant where we were to meet.

Hope soon appeared, but she held me at arm's length when I reached to give her a hug.

"No, don't touch!" she shouted softly. "Unclean!"

Then I got my first glimpse of Hope's eyes behind the frames of her wire-rimmed glasses, framed by her long city-girl brown hair. They were barely open, rather mole-like in fact, but what I could see of them was scarlet and watery.

With a pitiful sniff, she looked up at me through the red slits that were once blue eyes and asked, "Do you think anyone will notice?"

"Nahhhh," I lied.

"Becky, I think I may have an eye infection."

"No!" I said in mock surprise, then my maternal instincts kicked in. "Hope, we are going to have to get you to a doctor for antibiotic drops."

"But I'm starving," she said, "Let's eat first."

Thirty minutes later, we were conversing over a plate of beautifully-prepared food—not that Hope could see any of it.

Over dinner, Hope and I went from acquaintances to friends—bound by the question of how we were going to secure medicine for her late on a Sunday night in a big strange city, and by a delightful discovery of our love (obsession?) for well-written books. The kind of books that stand out like pieces of gold in a chest full of pennies. The sort of books that are found in the aisle far away from the brightest, newest, best-sellers. We discovered neither of us likes fiction much—we want to know that the stories we read actually happened to real, live people. But real-life stories cannot be told willy-nilly either—they need to be crafted with wit and tenderness and insight and honesty.

It also helps, we decided, if we read our cherished volumes in some book-enhancing environment, a place and time where one can savor the words like fine chocolate.

After dinner we drove around until we found an emergency room—conveniently across from the hotel where I was staying. I dropped Hope at the double doors of the hospital ER. Within a few minutes she ran out to the car to tell me it would probably be about a two-hour wait. Since I couldn't find a place to park in the dark I had no choice but to leave Hope at the mercy of the emergency room, with my cell phone for protection, while I went to my hotel and watched a movie and ordered room service—a to-die-for chocolate torte—and awaited Hope's call for me to come pick her up. (She still teases me about "abandoning her" in the antiseptic linoleum-ville while I ate cake in luxurious comfort, but what could I do?)

A week later, I returned to my home and Hope to hers. I could not resist writing to ask if she'd flown home on a "red-eye" special. That started our e-correspondence, and it's become a conversation that picks up and flies back and forth for a few days, then simmers down to nothing as we get back to work deadlines and the flurry of family. Then some thought or insight or a newly-discovered literary treasure starts the conversation flowing with fresh streams of rushing words. I saved the following e-mail and printed it out to take on my next visit to a bookstore. It captures, spontaneously and beautifully, the heart of a book lover.

> Oh, Becky…I was just thinking about you and how you asked about my favorite book titles last week. Okay, I am taking the long way to the list but hear me out.

We had a terrible return travel day from the convention. Terrible and delightful all at once...but one of our tour stops during our 13-hour delay in New Orleans was Barnes & Noble. And as we were wandering, I found some wonderful books by Mary Cantwell—released in a paperback compilation—and I thought of you, my little injured-wing friend. (How's the broken arm doing?)

Another favorite author: Helene Hanff who wrote *84 Charing Cross Road*, which is also a movie with Anne Bancroft and Anthony Hopkins. Book is good but the movie is lovely...

BUT I have got to tell you, Becky-my-becky, of the book I purchased just over a month ago and saved for the convention. It is called *Daybook* by Anne Truitt. She is an artist, a sculptor, and a painter, and *Daybook* has her journal entries over several significant times in her life. I cannot tell you...oh, yes I can...how INCRED-IBLE the writing is. It makes me weep and reflect on my life on a deeper level that allows for texture and color to be a part of that reflection. I mean it. I read portions of it out loud to Kari (my convention roomie) and she had the same feeling about it. I'm recom-mending it to everyone. She has two other memoirs, which I am ordering this week. I have never read writing as true and powerful as this and it is merely a woman speaking as a mother, an artist, and of course as a woman. Amazing stuff. And because they are journal entries she flows from topic to topic, which means that you can leave it to go play in the summer sun and THEN return to a shiny new perfect-on-its-own entry. None of the "What in the world was going on last time I read this chapter?"

I am in this mode in life where I hunger for riches found in the experiences of others (other women mainly) as I seek the richness in my own experience.

Memoirs and well-written fiction on occasion feed my soul. It is as if I cannot get enough of these narrative voices that offer connection and inspiration and a look at how complex and simple we all are. I think I like such things because as my eyes follow the left to right pattern across the page my mind tumbles along screaming, "I am not a freak after-all!" The shared human experience does much to affirm my faith in God.

Peace to you and happy reading. If I think of any of the others...I will pass them on in a follow up email...much shorter I promise.

—H

Funny, as I read Hope's thoughts pouring across the miles, I had a sudden hankering for seafood linguini and Caesar salad (sans the red eyes) and a long conversation about books.

I started to e-mail her back, but before I got to the "create mail" button, this delightful postscript came in.

Becky,

One more thought. My gift to you...I offer a completely perfect afternoon with these last details:

While you are reading one of these books, I think it best to sip a Diet Coke with lime over crushed ice while listening to your favorite CD. Do you have a roof deck? That would really be ideal.

Oooohhhh wait...I just remembered, this is YOU, Becky—for pete's sake! I can see the headlines, "Successful young author...last words... 'Hope told me to read on the roof for a complete....experience...ugh.'"

On second thought, forget the roof, Becky.

—Hope

Now this is a bookaholic after my own heart. (I'm benevolently overlooking, of course, the little joke about my clutziness and the roof.) But really, when a friend not only recommends titles, but tells you where you should read them, the beverage to sip, and the music to play in the background—well, I ask you, does a book pal get any better than this?

I think not.

In fact, Hope's message got me thinking about books I've loved and read in special places, especially the volumes I could take time to savor that met a deep emotional need. I can almost name the years by a book title that challenged, changed, or soothed my soul.

Roaring Lambs was such a book-of-the-year for me.

Two of my favorite soul-lifting books were read near the wild comfort of ocean waves. I can almost feel and smell the warm salty sea-breezes and hear the sound of ships mingled with seagulls' calls as I opened the pages of Anne Morrow Lindbergh's classic, *Gift from the Sea*. I could not believe that someone who had lived so many decades before me, and who had survived the tragedy of her young son's kidnapping and death, could speak so relevantly to my own heart about slowing down and enjoying each moment.

The next year's inspirational seaside read was Arthur Gordon's collection of inspirational stories, *A Touch of*

Wonder. I suppose I've quoted from Mr. Gordon more than from any other writer. He catches the flavor of the South and humanity as a whole in a way that always charms, amuses, and lifts my spirits.

Philip Yancey has been a true elder brother to me through his books—and his occasional personal notes—freeing me from remnants of legalism in *What's So Amazing About Grace*, and painting Jesus so completely in *The Jesus I Never Knew* that I fell in love with Christ anew, never to return to my old way of seeing Him. In fact, I remember the very moment I finished the last words on the last page of *The Jesus I Never Knew* though I can't honestly say I remember the actual words. I just remember the feeling was one of sun-splashed joy, gold-tinged by grace.

I was sitting in a hotel room in Nashville, enjoying a quiet breakfast on a Sunday morning near an open window. The sun warmed the open pages as I read slowly, drinking the words into my parched soul. I was far from home and missing my family, but I wasn't lonely. I had a friend, an author, speaking to me, chatting with me, sharing from the depths of his soul about the person of Jesus Christ, the Messiah, transformed in Philip's mind from a milky white picture on a Sunday school paper to Love-Made-Flesh—a God who flung the stars into space who was still intimate enough to cook up a mess of fish for His friends.

As I finished the last word, church bells began to chime in the distance, and I felt enveloped by Christ Himself, lost in His love in a private but holy moment.

Brenda Waggoner's book, *The Velveteen Woman*, along with Brenda's own "realness" left permanent footprints (rabbit prints?) on my heart. What a privilege it was to read Brenda's manuscript pages, to be a part of her work-in-progress even before we found a publisher. I just got off the phone with Lee Hough, her editor on this project. He told me that when he read my chapter on "Guy Friends" in this book, he could only think of a line from the movie, *As Good As It Gets*. "Reading this makes me want to be a better man." I feel this way about Brenda and her work. Knowing her as my friend, reading her work, and listening to her talk makes me want to be a better woman—more open, more compassionate, but most of all—more real.

It was Lee who recommended Brennan Manning's books to me and Brenda. *Ragamuffin Gospel. Abba's Child*. Books that talk so openly about Brennan's brush with failure, his struggles as an alcoholic, and the Christ who loves him anyway. I chuckled aloud at one of his lines about facing the truth about who he really was as a man: an angel with an enormous capacity for beer. In that image, he captured the uneasy truth about who I really am as well. A woman with the love of God pulsing through her veins, one who battles a shadow side as surely all of us do on this side of eternity.

So many books I have enjoyed have been gifts from friends. It was Brenda who gave my husband *The Sacred Romance* by Brent Curtis and John Eldridge for his birthday—a book that would change the mental course of Scott's life. I could see his brow unfurrow, the lines in his face relax as he soaked up chapter after chapter. Scott's not much of a reader, so I was amused to watch him carry the worn paperback around like a puppy for days at a time. When I could finally get Scott to let go of it for my turn at reading (and trust me it took some hard tugging), I found myself equally absorbed.

We loved the message and its authors, whose hearts were laid bare on every page. Brent and John seemed to have a friendship much like David and Jonathan's. More than brothers, they were kindred spirits.

I'll never forget the morning I was sitting in a little restaurant having breakfast in Fredericksburg, Texas—a quaint little German town—interviewing Suzie Humphries for my book, *Real Magnolias.* One of her friends came up to our table and said, "Suzie, you've got to read this book called *The Sacred Romance.*" I looked up at Suzie's friend in delight and, over the mutual love of a book, we had instant connection. Then she said something that made me recoil inside, as if I'd been kicked unaware by something horrible and unreal. "Becky," the woman said kindly, "did you hear that Brent died in a rock-climbing accident this month?"

No, I had not. And though I never met Brent, I felt as though I had. Because he had touched and profoundly changed my husband's heart, and my own husband is a rock climber (we even have a rock climbing wall in our HOUSE), it was like hearing Scott's friend had suddenly died. I carried the news home and unwrapped it gently, the way one would carefully unwrap the broken pieces of a cherished heirloom, as I shared the tragedy with Scott. He took it hard. There were tears shed on our dock that night as the sun went down, for a friend my husband would never meet this side of heaven, but one he had loved anyway.

Such is the power of a writer's words. So when women write me and say, "Becky, I feel as though we are friends, as though we've known each other somehow," I know how they feel, and do not take for granted the gift of their caring and reaching out to me. For books and their writers, if they touch our lives, do indeed on some level become our friends.

This weekend I was finally able to pick up one of the books Hope recommended, *84 Charing Cross Road* by Helene Hanff. (As I paid for my purchase, the Barnes & Noble employee handed it to me and said, "Oh, I love this book. Have you seen the movie?" Guess what video I'll be renting this weekend?) *Charing Cross* is the consummate booklover's read: actual correspondence, over a 20-year period, between a writer/booklover from New York and the owner of a bookshop (imagine the quaint shop in *You've Got Mail*) in London during the lean post-war years. The New Yorker is a sharp-witted American working on breaking through the British reserve of the shop's manager, and it makes for some hilarious reading.

> Dear Frank...
>
> My dear little dentist...went on his honeymoon. I financed the honeymoon. Did I tell you he told me last spring I had to have all my teeth capped or all my teeth out? I decided to have them capped as I have got used to having teeth. But the cost is simply astronomical.... I do NOT intend to stop buying books, however, you have to have SOMEthing. ... now, listen, Frankie, it's going to be a long cold winter and I baby-sit in the evenings AND I NEED READING MATTER, NOW. DON'T START SITTING AROUND, GO FIND ME SOME BOOKS. hh [9]

Only a fellow bookworm could understand the logic of why we would rather cut back on groceries, go without a new dress, and drive an old car than give up our books. Books get us through lean times, cold times, trying times, and good times. They are our reward for putting up with long days.

If you are blessed enough, as a booklover, to meet another book friend—you will never run out of conversational topics. If one of you gets a delicious read, you treat it as you would the perfect slice of cheesecake in the company of friends. After taking a bite and deciding it's too wonderful to keep to yourself, you pass over the fork and plate—or in this case, the book—for your friend's literary tasting enjoyment.

In fact, my reward for finishing the writing of this book is Hope's latest list of recommendations.

Yes, my reward for *writing* is always *reading*. (Scott cannot believe that I've not yet exhausted my interest in words: spoken, written, or read. I feel the same thing about his interest in fishing: bass, perch, and trout.)

Enough rambling and writing for today.

If you will excuse me, my fellow reading friend, I have an appointment on the roof with a new book, a CD, and a lime cola.

> *And there are also many other things that Jesus did,*
> *which if they written one by one, I suppose*
> *that even the world itself could not contain*
> *the books that would be written. Amen.*
> JOHN 21:25 NKJV

"*The one thing I regret is that*
I will never have time to read
all the books I want to read."
—Francoise Sagan

Becky's Favorite Book Quote of the Year

After a much too busy spring (again!), I found myself seaside for emotional and spiritual repairs. I wandered into an out-of-the-way bookshop that even smelled of salty wisdom. I pulled out this tiny, dusty volume called *Serenity Is*.... Flipping through the pages I found a quote that touched a chord so deep in my soul that I felt like singing, "This is true! This is the way I'm longing to live!"

I offer it to you, my bookworm friends, as MY gift. (I suggest reading it on a porch swing with the sun pouring over your shoulder, Pachelbel's Canon playing in the background, a glass of freshly brewed iced tea with a mint leaf in it near you.)

The best things in life move slowly. They can hardly overtake one who is in a hurry. We are making haste to ill purpose if we "haven't time" to read good books, to think quietly, to visit our friend, to comfort the sick and sorrowing, to enjoy the beautiful creations of God and man, and to lend a hand to a struggling brother. Time is precious, but more precious than fleeting hours are truth, love, benevolence, friendship, service, a serene mind and a happy heart, for these are the essence of life itself.[10]

Thoughts on Reading & Writing
from Women Writers

"I read constantly. If I don't have a good book, I'm beside myself."

—Gail Godwin

"When you reach out and touch other human beings, it doesn't matter whether you call it therapy or teaching or poetry."

—Audre Lorde

"You can't clobber any reader while he's looking. You divert his attention, then you clobber him and he never knows what hit him."

—Flannery O'Conner

"It's very difficult to be married and write, to be unmarried and write, to have children or not have children and write."

—Laurel Speer

"I just flat out announce I'm working, leave me alone and get out of my face. When I 'surface' again, I try to apply poultice and patch up the holes I've left in relationships around me. That's as much as I know to do...so far."

—Toni Cade Bambara

Scone Muffins

Scones for Munching on a Reading Afternoon

(This recipe makes the tastiest scones I've ever had. Melissa Gantt, my chick flick friend, once telephoned me and asked if I would walk over to her back porch for a visit. With classical music playing around us and the sparkling lake before us, she served me these wonderful scones, complete with hot tea.)

1 c. flour
½ t. baking soda
1 t. baking powder
1-2 T. sugar
¼ t. salt
½ c. cold butter, cut into small chunks
1-1¼ c. buttermilk
1 c. Craisins (dried sweetened, cranberries—near the raisins in the grocery store)

Grease or Pam a muffin tin, (or mini-muffin tins). Preheat oven to 375 degrees. Sift flour, baking powder, baking soda, sugar and salt into bowl.

Cut in butter until flour mixture resembles cornmeal. Don't overmix. Stir in buttermilk and add Craisins. The mixture will be very thick and will resemble biscuit batter. Drop by spoonfuls into muffin tin. Bake until slightly brown on top and until cake tester inserted comes out clean. Serve warm, with butter, if desired. Also good with ½ c. nuts.

A reader friend sent me this poem that sums up the sort of friend I wish for each of you! When I wrote to the author for permission to print the poem, I discovered that it was based on a friend of the author, Mildred Doxtader, who will be 82 on her next birthday!

More Whipped Cream[11]

I have a new delightful friend,
I'm almost in awe of her;
When we first met I was impressed,
By her bizarre behavior.
That day I had a date with friends,
We met to have some lunch;
Mae had come along with them,
All in all...a pleasant bunch.

When the menus were presented,
We ordered salads, sandwiches, and soups;
Except for Mae who circumvented,
And said, "Ice-cream, please. Two scoops."
I was not sure my ears heard right,
And the others were aghast;
"Along with heated apple pie,"
Mae smiled, completely unabashed.

We tried to act quite nonchalant,
As if people did this all the time;
But when our orders were brought out,
I did not enjoy mine.
I could not take my eyes off Mae,
As her pie a la mode went down;
The other ladies showed dismay,
They ate their lunches, and they frowned.

Well, the next time I went out to eat,
I called and invited Mae;
My lunch contained white tuna meat,
She ordered a parfait.
I smiled when her dish I viewed,
She asked if she amused me;
I answered, "Yes, you do,
And you also do confuse me.

"How come you order rich desserts
When I feel I must be sensible?"
She laughed and said, with wanton mirth,
"I am tasting all that's possible.
I try to eat the food I need,
And do the things I should;
But life's so short, my friend, indeed,
I hate missing out on something good.

"This year I realized I was old,"
She grinned, "I've not been this old before;
So, before I die, I've got to try,
Those things for years I have ignored.
I've not smelled all the flowers yet,
And too many books I have not read;
There's more fudge sundaes to wolf down,
And kites to be flown overhead.

"There's many malls I have not shopped,
I've not laughed at all the jokes;
I've missed a lot of Broadway hits,
And potato chips and Cokes.
I want to wade again in water,
And feel ocean spray upon my face;
Sit in a country church once more,
And thank God for His grace.

"I want peanut butter every day,
Spread on my morning toast;
I want untimed long-distance calls,
To the folks I love the most.
I've not cried at all the movies yet,
Nor walked in the morning rain;
I need to feel wind in my hair,
I want to fall in love again.

"So, if I choose to have dessert,
Instead of having dinner;
If I should die before nightfall,
You'd have to say I died a winner.
That I missed out on nothing,
That I had my heart's desire;
That I had that final chocolate mousse,
Before my life expired."

With that, I called the waitress over,
"I've changed my mind, it seems;"
I said, "I want what she is having,
Only add some more whipped cream."

A Final Word:

The Friend You've Always Dreamed Of

I'm much more of a day dreamer than a night dreamer, but I once had a night dream—so vivid and so real—that I woke up feeling as if I'd gone away and come back to earth with a bit of heaven tucked in the palm of my hand. Whether it was just a dream that was symbolic to me, personally, or a gift-dream from the Lord's heart to my soul, I do not know. I share it with you as one who is wary of people who say, "God told me this" or "The Lord gave me a dream"—as one who believes that in unexpected moments, God does indeed give His children personal glimpses of Himself, His goodness, His merciful nature. It's the way of a good friend to do that on occasion. And so, this was my dream...

I was walking along a beach, barefooted, when a young man with dark curly hair came up and asked me to dance. I assumed, by his looks, that he was Italian. "But I have no shoes," I told him. "Will you walk with me back to the house so I can get them?"

And as we walked along the beach, I looked into his eyes and had the strangest feeling that I was looking at someone who knew me better than I knew myself. He had the wisdom of a father, the easy camaraderie of a brother or a close friend, and the intimate knowing of my naked soul, like a loving husband. The longer we talked, the more at ease I felt in the presence of such kindness and acceptance, the more completely myself.

We passed by all the people I knew and loved the most—my parents, my children, my husband—and I waved to each of them, introducing them to my friend.

When we arrived in front of my house, I asked my new friend if he was Italian.

"No," he said, "I am Jewish."

I nodded, then turned to go get my shoes.

"Wait," he said, holding out his arms. "You'll not need your shoes to dance with Me." I looked in those incredible eyes once again, then I caught my breath—for I knew He was no ordinary man. And indeed, there was no need for shoes, because I was standing on Holy Ground.

I awoke from that dream, but I've never been quite the same since.

I had been in the presence of Someone who saw me as I really was, only He filtered everything—the good, bad, and ugly—through His eyes of love.

In my dream, I waltzed with the Friend of friends, the Lover of My Soul, under the very stars He had once flung into space.

And now, even in the light of day, I dream of the time I will lean on the everlasting arms again, dancing to the music of angels, lost in the warmth of His love.

*Were not our hearts burning within us
while he talked with us on the road?*
LUKE 24:32

"Draw all the closer to Me; come,
flee unto Me to hide thee, even from thyself.
Tell Me about the trouble. Trust Me to turn My hand
upon thee and thoroughly to remove the boulder
that has choked thy riverbed....Fear thou not,
O child of My love; fear not."
—Amy Carmichael

Recipe for Communion
with Christ

Unleavened bread, pure, white, broken as His body was broken for you and for me.

Wine, red, as a symbol of the blood it cost our Savior to rescue us from Satan's evil grip and bring us safely to the Father's side.

Eat. Sip. Share. Remember.

...Jesus took bread, gave thanks and broke it, and gave it to his disciples, saying, "Take and eat; this is my body." Then he took the cup, gave thanks and offered it to them, saying, "Drink from it, all of you. This is my blood of the covenant, which is poured out for many for the forgiveness of sins."
MATTHEW 26:26-28

"Greater love has no one than this, that he lay down his life for his friends."
—John 15:13

The End

Notes

1. Candace B.. Pert, *Your Body Is Your Subconscious Mind* (Sounds True, 2000).
2. Source: Internet
3. Source: Internet
4. Source: Internet
5. Faith Popcorn, et al., *EVEolution: The Eight Truths of Marketing to Women* (Hyperion, 2000).
6. Susan J. Jeffers, *Feel the Fear and Do It Anyway* (Fawcett, 1992).
7. Terry Hershey, *Go Away, Come Closer: When What You Need the Most Is What You Fear the Most* (Hershey & Associates, 1990).
8. Dr. Paul Pearsall, *The Pleasure Prescription* (Hunter House, 1996).
9. Helene Hanff, *84 Charing Cross Road* (Penguin USA, 1990).
10. Gilbert Hay, compiler, *Serenity Is...* (Simon & Schuster, 1969).
11. Virginia Ellis, *More Whipped Cream* (c. 2000), used by permission. More poems by this author can be found at: www.geocities.com/heartland/creek/7984/index.html or http://members.aol.com/mempenny4/ginny.html

❖ ❖ ❖

For information about Becky's other books
and speaking schedule, check out her Web
site at www.beckyfreeman.com.

E-mail Gene Kent at speakupinc@aol.com
for information about having Becky speak
at your retreat, conference, or special event.

❖ ❖ ❖

Vanilla, Strawberry, or Chocolate Chili Pepper?

Becky Freeman is famous for observing (and experiencing) the crazy and compassionate, the delight and doubt, and the love and laughter of life. Chocolate Chili Pepper Love is a heartwarming collection of fun ideas and hilarious tales that will bring smiles of joy and a new perspective to your marriage.

Discover:

- the differences between an easy "vanilla" marriage, a fun "strawberry" marriage, and the excitement of a "chocolate–chili pepper" marriage
- the keys to making a high-maintenance relationship successful
- how to have fun even in the difficult times

Finding a good dose of humor and hope amid the clutter of kids and romantic moments gone wrong, Becky reminds you that marriage is a journey to be celebrated.

Other Books Authored or Coauthored
by Becky Freeman

Chocolate Chili Pepper Love

Peanut Butter Kisses & Mud Pie Hugs

Worms in My Tea and Other Mixed Blessings

Adult Children of Fairly Functional Parents

Marriage 911

Still Lickin' the Spoon

A View from the Porch Swing

Real Magnolias

Courage for the Chicken Hearted

Egg-stra Courage for the Chicken Hearted

Available from your local Christian bookstore